MADE RIGHTEOUS THROUGH FAITH

Timothy D. Marsh

Made Righteous Through Faith

Timothy D. Marsh

Copyright 2013 © by Timothy D. Marsh

ISBN 978-1-61529-104-5

Vision Publishing
1672 Main Street E 109
Ramona, CA 92065
1 800 9 VISION
www.booksbyvision.com

TABLE OF CONTENTS

Dedication

This book is dedicated to the praise and glory of our Lord and Savior Jesus Christ,

to my wonderful wife, Carole-Anne,

my four great children, David (gone to be with Jesus),

Julie-Anne, Jonathan, and Rebecca,

and to my grandchildren, Isaiah and Caleb.

God, always bless them and keep them in His care.

Also, special thanks to our good friend in the Gospel,

Marybeth Woodward,

for her contribution in writing this book.

For by

GRACE

are ye saved through faith,
and that not of yourselves;
it is the gift of God,
not of works,
lest any man should boast.

Ephesians 2:8-9

FORWARD

Some 500 years ago the great German Reformer, Martin Luther, changed the course of human history with his explosive sermons on justification by faith alone, apart from any work of ours. Entire nations were transformed by his powerful preaching. Nonetheless, there were aspects of the gospel that remained little known, or at least were neglected, until the middle of the last century. Then came an astonishing outburst of what could be called the "righteousness" message, or the "new creation," along with a fresh understanding of the power of personal faith, especially when it is linked with the Word of God and with the name of Jesus. Millions of lives worldwide have been, and are being, transformed by this latter day revelation. If the focus of the Reformation was "justification", then in our time the Holy Spirit has brought a new focus, full of laughter and spiritual triumph – "righteousness!"

Tim Marsh has taken up that great theme and created this remarkably readable book. Here you will find clear exposition of some of the most amazing ideas in the New Testament, matched with many anecdotes that apply those ideas to daily life. Hence this is not just a book of theory, but rather a practical guide on how to live each day enjoyably, victoriously, and prosperously in Christ. Tim also shows the enormous potential of your own faith in God, how to link that faith to God's promises, and how to move mountains and change your world by speaking the name of Jesus. And throughout he maintains a wise balance, avoiding the extremes that some have urged. This is a book to be read with delight. You may well never be the same again!

Ken D. Chant, M.R.E: Ph.D.

The familiar saying, "The pen is mightier than the sword" can be applied to what Tim Marsh has written in the book titled "Made Righteous Through Faith." In the following lines, you will be given a clear, easy to read, and precise reason for Christ's disciples to "Beat their swords into plow shares, and their spears into pruning hooks."

The pen of a God-inspired writer speaks truth that sets people free. The struggle to achieve righteousness by the works of the law has been a long drawn-out warfare that ends at the cross. The struggle to become "righteous enough to please a Holy God by works-of-the-Law-keeping" ends up in futility. Once a hungry soul realizes that "He who knew no sin was made sin for us that we might be made the righteousness of God," his battle for righteousness ends in victory.

The old filthy rags of self-righteousness can be laid aside, and now one can wear the robe of God's gift of righteousness. It would be wrong for one to believe that "all God-inspired writings" ceased when the last lines of the book of Revelation were written, when there are still men of God who have a desire to see God's people set free from the struggle to become righteous and who are motivated by spiritual inspiration to write. I believe Tim Marsh to be among them. I firmly believe that the messages of God's righteousness that are found in his book "Made Righteous Through Faith" are able to assist the reader to cease from his own labors and enter into God's refreshing rest.

The need for the message contained in the following pages is of cosmic proportion. The release of God's presence and power is realized when the truth of God's gift of righteousness is experienced in one's life. The message of this book can be counted worthy of four positive appraisals. First: the fact that the book is scripturally sound and is easy reading. Second: the fact that Tim Marsh has written by inspiration. Third: the fact that the book is Biblically sound and contains continuity of thought on the subject matter, and can be used as a text book in a classroom setting for teaching the subject of righteousness. Fourth: the fact that the message written in the book is the heart and soul of a man of God who is motivated with a passion to assist the child of God in his quest for righteousness.

Of all the books I have read on the subject of faith and righteousness, Tim's book excels in scriptural fact and clarity of continuity.

Tim Marsh and his wife Carol-Anne come to us from the great land of Australia. They were converted under the ministry of Leo Harris, the apostolic founder of the great Christian Revival Crusade (CRC), out of which a number of great men of God birthed many churches in that country. Tim was personally mentored by Leo Harris who moved in deliverance ministry for many years, and was known and sought after by his own countrymen and throughout the world. Tim carries with him the attribute of that great ministry.

I highly recommend the reading of this book to all pastors and laity to whom this book might be introduced.

Dr. Joseph Thornton, Th.D.

INTRODUCTION

Everything about God is Amazing! Amazing love! Amazing grace! And Amazing truth! What an amazing revelation it is that God would declare us RIGHTEOUS BY FAITH, that by simple faith in His finished work on the cross we are MADE THE RIGHTEOUSNESS OF GOD IN HIM. How can it be? Yet it is true! There is nothing we can do to merit such KINDNESS AND MERCY. **"For by GRACE are you SAVED through FAITH, and that not of yourselves. It is the GIFT of God, not of works lest any man should boast (Ephesians 2:7).**

This amazing love can only be RECEIVED. It can't be earned or worked for. It can't be paid for with silver and gold. Our salvation has already been bought and paid for at the cross of Calvary. Friend, Calvary has you covered, today and for eternity. Your salvation is settled, delivered and signed for in the blood red ink of Calvary!

God never goes back on His Word. The assurance of your salvation is secure and backed up by His infallible Word. No man can pluck you out of His hand; you are His for keeps! Amen! Your redemption was bought with the precious blood of Jesus, therefore you are sealed of the Holy Spirit for eternity. PRAISE THE LORD!

You are no longer trying to be saved as He has already accepted you in the Beloved. He has placed you IN CHRIST, and blessed you in heavenly places. The abundance of His grace has pardoned all your sins and covered you with the garment of salvation and with the ROBE OF RIGHTEOUS-

NESS. Isn't that wonderful? And that is not all; it gets better. The BLOOD is SPEAKING on your behalf every moment of every day; you're under its cleansing flow declaring you, THE RIGHTEOUSNESS OF GOD IN HIM.

Many believers understand little of their God-given position of Righteousness. They are beset with inferiority, guilt, unworthiness and self-condemnation. The enemy reminds them constantly of their weakness and he steals their joy and robs them of their shout of victory. Their peace is confiscated and their Christian walk has lost its vitality.

Friend, we are not fighting _for_ the victory; we are fighting _from_ it. God is calling His people to an amazing life of joy and victory. Let go of the bondage of religion and frustration, and break through into the glorious liberty of the children of God. Let the striving, the turmoil, and the struggle go. Stop trying to be what you already are: THE RIGHTEOUSNESS OF GOD IN CHRIST. The enemy will cease his tactics when we get it settled. His blame game will not work when our feet are on the rock.

Let's get it right by knowing who we are and what God has made us. It is not until we settle the issue, that Jesus, and He alone, is our righteousness, that we can experience the peace of God that flows like a river. Break loose, child of God, and enjoy what you may be missing. You are who God says you are.

Timothy D. Marsh

Chapter One

MADE RIGHTEOUS THROUGH FAITH

One day while driving along a country road in the state of South Australia, I felt the prompting of the Holy Spirit to pull over and to pray. As I began to pray in the quietness of the country, the Spirit of the Lord came upon me. It just seemed like the heavens opened up and the Holy Spirit was poured out upon me – those times with the Lord are very real and precious! I can still remember looking at my watch as I went on my way, saying, "You were here for three hours." Someone said, "Time flies when you're having fun!"

The Holy Spirit is so wonderful as He knows what we have need of. My heart at the time was searching for the liberating truth of God's Word. For some reason, there was a personal struggle in my life and I needed to come into a greater revelation of God's rest.

During this country road experience, the Lord led me to Romans chapter seven where the Apostle Paul was dealing with his own struggle of trying to please God instead of trusting in the finished work of Jesus on the cross. Paul, in his search, came from endeavoring to make himself righteous by his own works, to the righteousness of Jesus Christ by faith.

He discovered that with all of his steadfastness and efforts to keep the Law, it still didn't make him righteous. It seemed the more he tried, the less he succeeded. God had to bring Paul to the end of himself as He does to each of us.

14

> "(that I may)...be found in Him, not having mine own **righteousness** which is of the Law, but that which is through the **faith** of Christ, the **righteousness** which is of God by faith"
>
> Phil. 3:8

Liberation came to Paul: the truth set him free. You can sense the conflict in his soul as he cried out to God for help. It has been an age-old problem of letting go so that God can take over. One day Paul's struggle to be made righteous came to an end. His spiritual eyes were opened. What he was trying to become, he discovered he already WAS by God's amazing grace. The turmoil was over when he discovered the battle had been won. Jesus had won the victory and there was nothing left to prove.

The Apostle Paul was a very zealous and ambitious character in upholding the laws of Israel, even to the point of error, but it all had to go! God had to bring this man to the place where he was nothing and Jesus was everything. Paul's personal reign of power was over; he was to die if Christ was to reign. That was hard for Paul, as Paul was always in charge. Now he is crying out for deliverance, **"Oh, wretched man that I am! Who shall deliver me from this body of death? . . . I thank God through Jesus Christ our Lord . . ." (Rom. 7:24-25).** Nothing is more glorious than when we come to the end of our puny efforts to be made righteous. Often it's not what one needs to learn, but rather what he needs to unlearn.

It is very hard for mankind to surrender their pride, but pride keeps people out of the Kingdom of God. Jesus called Zacchaeus down from the tree he was perched in. If we want Jesus to go home with us and have Him stay at our house, then we too must come down! When Paul was converted on the dusty road to Damascus, the Bible records that **"he fell to the ground" (Acts 9:4).**

Something of eternal value took place on that country road that day, not too far from the town of Port Augusta. My life was changed! I am glad that I listened to the Holy Spirit to stop the car that day. Sometimes our own plans need to be put on hold.

COMING FROM BENEATH THE LAW

Much is said today of the Ten Commandments yet they cannot save us in terms of giving us salvation. The Ten Commandments are good and righteous yet no one but Jesus has kept them. The Commandments serve to make us all guilty and in need of a Savior. They set a standard for good moral behavior for any people, but RIGHTEOUSNESS comes by JESUS CHRIST.

John explained, **" . . . the law was given by Moses, but <u>grace</u> and <u>truth</u> came by Jesus Christ" (John 1:17).** If you had to decide between the Commandments or grace and truth, which would you choose? The law brings with it guilt, death, and condemnation, always feeling bad, and never being good enough. Grace and truth bestow MERCY, FORGIVENESS, RIGHTEOUSNESS, and ACCEPTANCE.

The law of works represents a daily struggle, fear, and bondage. Many folk live under this heavy load when Jesus could set them free in an instant. Jesus said, **"Ye shall know the truth, and the truth shall make you free . . . If the Son therefore shall make you free, ye shall be free indeed" (John 8:32, 36).**

I Go to Prepare a Place

Jesus said, **"I go to prepare a place for you" (John 14:3).** Child of God, that place is a place of REST, a place of PEACE, a place of RIGHTEOUSNESS, a place of FREEDOM.

Why is it that people allow man to place heavy burdens on them? Jesus came to undo the heavy burdens and to let the OPPRESSED go free. He came to destroy the yoke of bondage. Are you under that load, my friend? If you are, you have not yet learned the truth! The truth is that Jesus did **"not come to destroy men's lives, but to save them" (Luke 9:56).** You can come into that place by simple FAITH in the Lord Jesus Christ. Make Him your Lord and Savior by giving your heart to Him.

Grace and truth will seat you in Heavenly places. How would you like that? It will lift you out of shame, self-condemnation, and unworthiness and will put you in Heavenly places in Christ Jesus. How would you like to be lifted up into Heavenly places with Jesus Christ and be seated with Him?

This Is the Believer's Position

". . . He hath raised us up together, and made us sit together (with Christ) in Heavenly places in Christ Jesus" (Eph. 2:6). Why would anyone trade this glorious place (position) for anything else? Why would anyone settle for religious bondage when they can have an experience with the living Christ?

A man asked his friend, "How are you today?" His friend answered, "I'm okay under the circumstances." His friend replied, "What are you doing under there?" The Word says, **"God shall make thee the head, and not the tail; and thou shalt be above only, and thou shalt not be beneath . . ." (Deut. 28:13).**

Let God's Grace Take Over

Grace is God's undeserved, intentional, extravagant favor. It is divine favor. You cannot earn, buy, or work for it. God's grace is free and post-paid! Grace is like a crown that is placed upon your head. The Psalmist said, **". . . who crowneth thee with <u>loving kindness</u> and <u>tender mercies</u>" (Ps. 103:4).

> **"For by grace are ye saved through faith, and that not of yourselves: it is the gift of God: not of works, lest any man should boast"**
>
> **Eph. 2:8-9**

Grace declares you **saved**.

Grace declares you **forgiven**.

Grace declares you **righteous**.

Grace declares you **justified**.

Grace declares you **sanctified**.

Grace declares you **accepted**.

Grace declares you a **child of God**.

A man once said to me, "You don't know how bad I've been." He said, "I've been so low I had to reach up to touch bottom." I replied, "God's arm is long enough to reach down into the lowest hell and rescue the worst of sinners." The Word of God declares, **"Where sin abounded, grace did much more abound" (Rom. 5:20).** You see, God is a "much more" God. The grace of God is unlimited. It knows no boundaries and has no exceptions.

Jesus Gave You the Gift of Righteousness

Having the gift of righteousness is having the right to come before Him without a sense of <u>guilt</u>, shame, inferiority, unworthiness, condemnation, or timidity. Righteousness is the believer's position that is bestowed upon him or her by the <u>faith</u> <u>of Jesus</u>. We cannot earn His righteousness by doing good things and religious practices. Righteousness is a free <u>gift</u>, rewarded by faith and by the <u>ABUNDANCE OF HIS GRACE.</u>

Let's see it from the Word of God. **"If by one man's offence (Adam) death reigned by one, <u>much more</u> they which receive <u>abundance of grace</u> and of the**

gift of righteousness shall reign in life by one, Jesus Christ" (Rom. 5:17).

Child of God, can you comprehend this phenomenon that your right-standing is a **gift of God?** This means that your faith is accounted to you for **righteousness.** You see, the Bible makes it clear that God is a REWARDER OF FAITH. Our perfect example is our father Abraham. God declared him RIGHTEOUS because he simply BELIEVED God. **"Abraham believed God, and it was accounted to him for righteousness" (Gal. 3:6).**

The word "accounted" is a mathematical term; e.g. 2+2=4 is a fact and unalterable. God has declared you righteous through the faith of Jesus. It cannot be altered, changed, or cancelled. Your position of righteousness is of God's doing. God said of David, **"My covenant will I not break, nor alter the thing that is gone out of My lips" (Ps. 89:34).**

Jeremiah Unveils Amazing Truth

This amazing truth is found in Jer. 23:5-6. **"Behold, the days come, saith the Lord, that I will raise unto David a righteous Branch, and a King shall reign and prosper . . . and this is His name whereby He shall be called, THE LORD OUR RIGHTEOUSNESS"** (Jesus).

The Greek word here for righteousness is *tsedeq* which means "all together" "to make right (in a moral and forensic sense." In other words, God has legally declared the believer all together righteous. When it comes to you, child of God, He left nothing out. Nothing was left undone. He made you **"the righteousness of God in Him" (2 Cor. 5:21).** Paul said it this way, **"We are complete (finished) in Him"** **(Col. 2:10).**

"If any man be <u>in Christ</u>, he <u>is</u> a NEW CREATION" (2 Cor. 5:14). The Word states that He <u>made</u> you the righteousness of God in Him. You are NOW a new creation. Your day has come; it has arrived, and you are <u>FOUND IN HIM</u>. He **"is <u>made</u> unto us WISDOM, RIGHTEOUSNESS, SANCTIFICATION, AND RE-DEMPTION" (1 Cor. 1:30).**

The enemy is clear out of the picture. He is defeated on the grounds of the finished work of Christ at the cross of Calvary. The claims of justice have been satisfied as the voice of the Father was heard, **"<u>This is My beloved Son in whom I am well pleased</u>" (Mt. 3:17; 17:5).**

The work of the cross was a finished work, and the pleasure of the Lord prospered in His hand. Jesus reigns triumphant over death, hell and the grave.

Friend, when we have Christ, we have the full package. Like the song said:

> All that I want is <u>Jesus</u>
> He satisfies, joy He supplies
> Life would be worthless without Him
> <u>All</u> <u>things</u> in Jesus I find.

Jeremiah stated, **"The King (Jesus) shall reign and prosper. . ." (Jer. 23:5).** This means you can reign and prosper too. **"(We) reign in life by one, Jesus Christ" (Rom. 5:17).** We are <u>not</u> a poor, struggling, defeated, wandering, aimless people. We are children of the living God, living victoriously by faith in His righteousness. We are not "half-baked," misplaced, and disgraced; we are the blood-washed, the Church, the redeemed.

It is time to come <u>boldly</u> to the throne of <u>GRACE</u>. It is time to shake off the intimidation of the enemy and stand firm in the <u>righteousness</u> He lavished on us through His unspeakable gift, Jesus.

"This is His Name whereby He shall be called, THE LORD OUR RIGHTOUSNESS" (Jer. 23:6).

God Made You His Righteousness

Righteousness did not just happen without a reason and a cause. Righteousness is fellowship with the Father and that is God's longing and desire: to meet with His children. Here is what He did: "**He (God) hath made Him (Jesus) to be sin for us, who knew no sin; that we might be made the righteousness of God in Him**" **(2 Cor. 5:21).**

Calvary and the work Jesus did there dealt with our sin problem, past, present, and future. He said, **"Your sins and iniquities will I remember no more" (Heb. 10:17).** If Jesus bore all of our sins for us, then they are all taken care of. We can't be charged with a single thing as Calvary covered it all. Isn't that wonderful?

If you had an outstanding debt you owed and your friend made the payment in full, your name would be cleared. Jesus cleared you at Calvary. You are no longer in debt; Jesus paid it all! He took your sin and nailed it to His cross and you can never be charged with it ever again.

A little girl was asked, "What do you do when the devil comes knocking?"

"Oh," she said, "I just let Jesus answer the door."

Jesus Made You Whole

Time after time, throughout the Gospels, Matthew, Mark, Luke and John, you read those miraculous words, **"Your faith has made you whole."** The Gospel makes us whole, and in particular, FAITH makes us whole **(Mt. 9:22),** i.e. faith in the finished work of the cross. The moment we BELIEVED, we were credited with His redemptive work. As quick as it took for you to say, "JESUS, SAVE ME," you were MADE WHOLE!

What does it mean to be MADE WHOLE? Let's take the word "whole" in its original language. It comes from the Greek word *"sozo"* meaning "safe," "to save," i.e. "deliver," "heal," "preserve," "do well," "to make whole."

When Jesus healed the sick, He did it instantly. The blind received their sight, the deaf were made to hear, the crippled walked, and the withered limbs were restored. These cases represent the spiritual needs of humanity. It only took an instant for the POWER OF GOD to deliver each one. The miracle took place right then and there.

YOUR BELIEVING FAITH COVERS YOU

> **"He hath clothed me with the garments of salvation, He hath covered me with the robe of righteousness"**
>
> **Is. 61:10**

Isaiah painted the picture for us. Child of God, see yourself as God sees you. All we need to do is look into the mirror of His Word. This is called the **"perfect law of liberty" (James 1:23-25).** We must look into the mirror of truth. The mirror cannot lie; it reveals the honest truth. Too many do not get the full picture and so they live only in part of the truth. The man or woman who BELIEVES what they see in the mirror walks in the law of liberty as one that has been delivered, healed, saved, and made whole.

Whenever a friend of mine finds expanded revelation from God's Word, he says, "I RECEIVE that!" May the Holy Spirit lead us into a deeper and fuller understanding of the finished work of the cross. We can only glory in what we know and have learned.

My friend, it is so important that we affirm the Word of God with a hearty "Amen!" We must agree with God by confessing it to be so. The Word exhorts us to **"Hold fast the profession of our faith without wavering (doubting)" (Heb. 10:23).** If the Word says that you have been made righteous - - - then you are! If the Word declares that you are more than a conqueror - - - then you are! If the Word states that you are a new creation in Him, then how can you be anything else? YOU ARE WHAT GOD SAYS YOU ARE!

If it takes nerve or faith to declare your position in Christ, do it anyway! It might turn it around for you; besides **"God calleth those things which are not as though they were" (Rom. 4:17).** God delights in you agreeing with Him. The natural mind wants to chew it over in view of finding God to be wrong. The natural mind sets up a barrier by questioning the Word of God, and the enemy wants to always confuse the issue. We resolve that by saying, **". . . let God be true, but every man a liar" (Rom. 3:4).**

The enemy has always tried to gainsay or contradict God's Word. Remember his tactics and subtlety in the Garden of Eden in how he beguiled (deceived) Eve. **"Now the serpent was more subtle than any beast of the field which the Lord God had made. And he said unto the woman, 'Yea, hath God said . . . ?" (Gen. 3:1)** Our adversary has never changed. He is still whispering in the ears of people, **"Hath God said?"**

Calvary Has You Covered

Let me ask you a question. Where is your faith centered? Some have their faith in their church, their organization, their religion, their good works, or just in themselves. This is a question that must be defined. It must be narrowed down to one thing and one thing alone and that is salvation through the cross of the Lord Jesus Christ.

I preached a funeral one time in a country town around the graveside. I sang with my guitar, "The Old Rugged Cross." The coldness I received from the undertakers was very noticeable. Up to that time, there was always an amiable friendship. Many are turning from the cross today as it doesn't coincide with their liberal gospel.

There is no salvation without the cross. There is redemption in nothing else than the blood that Jesus shed. To be saved, forgiven, and made whole comes about only by the cross of Christ. You can be up to your neck in religion all your life yet that will not save you. Some say there are many roads to God! You can't find that in my Bible, and I am sure it is not in yours. Jesus made it plain and simple. **"I am the way, the truth, and the life; no man cometh unto the Father, but by me" (John 14:6).**

The true believer lives in the shadow of the cross. He embraces its deliverance, its truth, and its redemption. The hymn writer said, ". . . nothing in my hand I bring; simply to the cross I cling."

The Cross Sets Us Free

The cross is where we laid our burden down. The burden of sin we carried for so many years was left at Calvary. The debt we owed was paid in full. It was there our burdened souls found liberty and where He turned our darkness into light.

I recently had a middle-aged man come forward to receive Christ. I led him to Christ and ministered to him for a time. He then began to laugh with the joy of the Lord. Jesus set him free! The anointing destroyed the yoke of bondage. The heaviness in his soul gave way to freedom. I tell you the delivering power of the cross does it every time.

Perhaps you are reading this and you are like this man. Why don't you take your burden to Calvary and leave it there? Sin is a crippling load to carry. You don't have to bear it one more minute. Take it to Calvary and get set free!

Who Are the Blessed?

The Word of God tells us, **"Blessed are they whose iniquities are forgiven, and whose sins are covered. Blessed is the man to whom the Lord will not impute sin" (Rom 4:7-8).** Take the word "impute." It means that God does not "take inventory of our sins" and He does not estimate or reckon it on our account. God doesn't have a check list, i.e. He is not keeping tabs on us, or keeping a count of anything. He is not critiquing us to get something on us, and He is not a fault-finder.

When the believer places himself under the shadow of the cross, the precious blood of Jesus speaks on his behalf, for the Spirit answers to the blood and tells us we are born of God. When you are in the cross, living within its covering, the Bible calls you BLESSED, meaning you are a BLESSED man or a BLESSED woman. The benefits of Calvary have you saved, healed, forgiven, washed, and redeemed. Tomorrow when you rise, declare that you are a BLESSED child of God.

One day it was raining and I invited a lady to share the umbrella I had with me. She accepted the offer and was very thankful she was able to stay dry. God has an umbrella of grace we can all come beneath. It is a shelter in a time of storm that keeps us from the elements of this world.

God said, "I will not impute sin"

How can this thing be? We must try and answer this anomaly with the prodigal's return. When the prodigal son came home, the father, without hesitation, put a NEW robe on his son with shoes on his feet, and a ring of reconciliation on his hand. He didn't deserve any of this, but GRACE wouldn't have it any other way. GRACE is God's undeserved favor!

The prodigal's father had every right to disown his son when you consider his hellacious and riotous living, yet the father wouldn't pay it any attention. The wayward son stank like a pig farm and looked like a stray dog yet his father was oblivious. The son said, "Just make me one of your hired servants," but the father was so overcome with gladness for his son's return he took no account of his son's mistakes. No inventory was taken, no estimates were made, and no sin was imputed. Isn't that just like our Heavenly Father? . . . That's the God I serve!

Have you ever observed such mercy? By the way, God's "forgetter" is so perfect He cannot remember what happened yesterday in your life. It is buried in the sea of His forgetfulness. **"(Your) sins and iniquities will I remember no more" (Heb. 10:17).** With all that said and out of the way, can you believe you are made a NEW CREATION, because that's who the Word says you are!

The Joy of His Rest

Wherever Jesus went, He brought rest to troubled hearts. One time Jesus saw His disciples in the midst of the sea, toiling in rowing for the wind was blowing very hard. When Jesus came to them, they marveled that the wind ceased. This is a picture of God bringing rest to His people **(Mark 6:48-51).** Jesus said, **"Come unto me, all ye that labour and are heavy laden and I will give you rest" (Mt. 11:28).**

"There remaineth therefore a rest to the people of God. For he that is entered into His rest, he also hath ceased from his own works, as God did from His. Let us labor therefore to enter into that rest" (Heb. 4:9-11).

The Old Testament covenant was characterized by doing the works of the law, works that were burdensome and demanding. However, the new covenant that Jesus made is one of righteousness by faith. It means that righteousness is obtained not by works of the law but by the faith of Jesus Christ. This truth is summed up in one verse, **"Christ is the end of the law for righteousness to every one that believeth" (Rom. 10:4).**

This sweet rest that Jesus speaks of is described by Isaiah, **"This is the rest wherewith ye may cause the weary to rest and this is the refreshing, yet they would not hear" (Is. 28:12).** There are scores of references referring to the believer's rest, more than we have time to mention. Can you get a glimpse of this blessed revelation? It doesn't mean that nothing is required of the believer anymore but it does mean that he or she has entered into a newfound rest, acknowledging that we are saved by His righteousness and not ours. It is not of works lest any man should boast.

Ephesians 2:6 tells us that He has raised us up together, and made us to SIT together in Heavenly places in Christ Jesus. Notice that it says, "He made us SIT together." The thought here is that one only sits down after the work is done! Well, the work IS done. Jesus cried out, **"It is finished" (John 19:30).** That word "finished" means "complete." We can now say, **"I am complete in Him" (Col. 2:10).**

Chapter Two

WHAT SHALL WE DO?

Some seeking Jews found Jesus and they said unto Him, **"'What shall we do, that we might work the works of God'? Jesus answered and said unto them, 'This is the work of God, that ye believe on Him (Jesus) whom He (God) hath sent'" (John 6:28-29).** It seems that mankind is obsessed with doing things to become something, yet in the Kingdom of God it is not about doing, but BELIEVING. These inquiring people asked the Master, "What shall we do?"

> **What we do is not the issue, but rather what we believe.**

Throughout the Gospel of John, the word "believe" is used 98 times. It makes you think, "God is trying to tell us something!" For what we do is not the issue, but rather what we believe. This Gospel of the Kingdom is not predicated on our good works and our performance but on the finished work He performed on the cross. In simple terminology, it's not what I can do, but what He has done!

THE KEY TO RIGHTEOUSNESS

Believing is our key to righteousness. Without our believing, our trust and reliance on Jesus for salvation, we have it in reverse. Wouldn't it be terrible to go a lifetime wondering if I had done enough good works to give me a home in Heaven? The Bible is clear, **"All our righteousnesses are as filthy rags" (Is. 64:6).** It is easy to understand that our righteousness is not going to work! So then, the only solution is to accept God's righteousness by the faith of Jesus Christ.

God imputes His righteousness to every BELIEVER. So is it going to be His righteousness or ours? Believing in the Son of God accredits us with His righteousness. If righteousness was obtained by our works and deeds, we would never have any boldness to come into His presence as we would not know if we had done enough good things. You see, that is where faith comes into the picture. Faith embraces His FINISHED WORK on our behalf.

What an awesome Savior we serve. He took all of our sins and buried them the sea of His forgetfulness, and He made us NEW CREATURES in Christ. Jesus became sin for us that we might be made the RIGHTEOUSNESS OF GOD IN CHRIST! We can endeavor to try and please God to gain His acceptance, but the epitome of God's pleasure is when we BELIEVE and RECEIVE.

GOOD WORKS ARE THE RESULT OF RIGHTEOUSNESS

One might say that this way of thinking cancels out any need to do good works. No, that is hardly the case! The good works of the believer become the result of our position of righteousness. Jesus went about doing good and healing all that were oppressed. We are not doing the works of Jesus to become righteous; that is already established through the new birth. We are doing them in response to the reigning of His righteousness within our hearts.

> **Isn't it time we begin to affirm the wonderful, unspeakable gift of His righteousness?**

It would be superfluous to try and work for something you already have. Isn't it time we begin to affirm the wonderful, unspeakable gift of His righteousness? When you get a moment, lift your hands and express your praise that you are the righteousness of God in Christ.

Establish this blessed truth in your life. The impact will set you free, and it might even set your feet a-dancin'!

WORKING FROM A PLACE OF REST

To some Christians, the believer's daily walk is one of feeling inadequate and incomplete. The truth is our victory is in our BELIEVING. **"If thou canst believe, all things are possible" (Mark 9:23).** Believing is our key to the blessings of God. We can take it further by saying BELIEVING the promises of God. There's power in His exceeding, great, precious promises. Those who BELIEVE the promises inherit the land. Believing moves the hand of God. It turns the wheels of FAITH, and when faith goes into action, God is praised.

Believing is affirming what God has said in His Word; it is believing the report. The master key of faith is in your hand, and when put into the lock and turned, the door will open.

What is your confession, dear friend? Is it "I BELIEVE?" The next time you're up against it, address the situation with "I believe God!" God DELIGHTS in us when we BELIEVE, trust, adhere, cling to His Word. THAT IS DOING THE WORKS OF GOD!

You will set a new course, becoming a believer. Nothing can stand in your way; nothing will be impossible. Instead of saying "I doubt it," say "I believe it!" Instead of declaring "I can't," say "I can, in Jesus' Name!"

Believe in who you are. You have been **"made the Righteousness of God, in Him (Christ)" (2 Cor. 5:21). "If God be for you, then who can be against you?" (Rom. 8:31).** Believe you are an overcomer and that through Christ you can do all things.

THE LANGUAGE OF RIGHTEOUSNESS

Righteousness has a language of its own. Every believer comes into the Kingdom of Light which is the kingdom of Righteousness. It is the realm of the **new man** or the realm of the **new creation. "The righteousness which is of faith speaketh" (Rom. 10:6)** It has a vocabulary and voice of its own. Our conversation is now directed in righteousness. Gone are the words of doubt, fear, and unbelief. Our words are now seasoned with faith and a good report.

The Word Was in My Tongue

Faith has an "I believe" confession. **"For the Word is nigh thee, even in thy mouth, and in thy heart, that is, the Word of faith which we preach" (Rom. 10:8).**

David said, **"I believed, therefore have I spoken" (Ps. 116:10).** Let me quote another statement of David, **"The Spirit of the Lord spake by me, and His word was in my tongue" (2 Sam. 23:2).** Think of that, the Word being in your mouth and in your tongue. Isaiah said that a seraphim took a live coal from off the altar of God with the tongs **"and he laid it upon my mouth, and said, 'Lo, this hath touched thy lips'" (Is. 6:7).** The fire of the Holy Spirit anointed his lips. Oh, this is what we need today in our pulpits, men and women who speak the oracle of God, words of power, words of fire right from the throne of God.

Do you see it, child of God? Never mind what others say. The spoken Word of God on your lips can transform your life. The confession of your faith means "to say the same thing."

Jeremiah was a mighty prophet of God, yet for some reason he refrained from delivering his message to the people. As time went by, this is what he said, **"Then I said, 'I will not make mention of Him, nor speak anymore in His Name.' But His word was in mine heart as a burning** fire shut up in my bones, and I was weary of forbearing (holding it back), and I could not" (Jer. 20:9).

Jeremiah stated, **His word was SHUT UP in my bones."** We must release the Word if it is going to do its work. It is not to be SHUT UP or just enclosed within. Let it out, speak it, do not hold it in. Turn the Word of righteousness loose in your life, let it go. It will release the power of God.

God Is Not Far Away

We are not to say, **"'Who shall ascend into Heaven?' (that is, to bring Christ down from above) or 'Who shall descend into the deep?' (that is, to bring up Christ again from the dead). But what saith it? 'The Word is nigh thee, even in thy mouth, and in thy heart': that is, the <u>Word of faith</u> which we preach" (Rom. 10:6-8).** Friend, God has already spoken, and He is as far away as the words of your mouth. He is made nigh to us when we believe and confess His Word.

Confession Brings Possession

You might be thinking, "I have heard this before!" It might be that some have taken the truth too far. However, there is a power in speaking the Word that compares with nothing else. I want to remind you again of the words of David, the Psalmist. **"I believed, therefore have I spoken" (Ps. 116:10).** Notice that Paul, in his second letter to the Corinthians quotes the same verse. **"We, having the same spirit of faith, according as it is written, 'I believed and therefore have I spoken,' we also believe and therefore speak" (2 Cor. 4:13).**

Believing and speaking the Word is a powerful combination. We are not referring to being a parrot with just words pouring out of our mouths, but professing and affirming the

Word in our lives. It is one thing to believe you love someone, yet another to confess it to be so.

Confessing you love them makes a statement of fact. When you think about it, the Word of God is God's confession to us; this is the reason we say, "Amen!"

> **The key to the blessing of God is to say what God says about you.**

When God says that you are a new creature in Christ, believe it and say so. **"Let the redeemed of the Lord say so, whom He hath redeemed from the hand of the enemy" (Ps. 107:2).**

The key to the blessing of God is to say what God says about you. It is not what you feel or even think; it is what the Word says. Don't reason with God but take Him at His Word. Agree with God and praise Him for His favor upon you. When God shares a wonderful truth with you, get happy about it and claim it for your own.

Chapter Three

GOD ESTABLISHED YOU IN RIGHTEOUSNESS

> **"In righteousness shalt thou be established!"**
>
> **Is. 54:14**

Here Is what the written Word declares: **". . . In righteousness shalt thou be established, thou shalt be far from oppression, for thou shalt not fear, and from terror, for it shall not come near thee" (Is. 54:14).**

"In **righteousness shalt thou be established!"** That sounds rather permanent, don't you think? The word "establish" means to be fixed, to render sure, to frame, to erect. This awesome position that God has given the believer embraces all of these objectives. Our position of righteousness is rock-solid and built sure upon the foundation of His redemption. The hymn writer wrote, "On Christ the solid rock I stand, all other ground is sinking sand."

The gift of God's righteousness is not something we have today and it is gone tomorrow. His righteousness is a permanent fixture. The believer is framed in His righteousness and put on display for the world to see.

Someone asked if a believer can lose this divinely imparted gift. How far does he have to go to forfeit such a trophy of amazing grace? Only God can answer that question, but who is thinking of that? Why should one ever entertain the thought of doing despite (insult) unto the Spirit of Grace?

What a tragedy it would be to trod underfoot the Son of God once one had known Him.

We do know that God's amazing grace has saved us and it keeps us day by day. The sinless blood of Jesus has the believer covered, safe and secure, while he ever makes Jesus Lord. Being a child of God does not mean that he doesn't make mistakes or cannot falter or fall. It means that goodness and mercy keeps following him all the days of his life.

YOU WERE GIVEN EVERLASTING LIFE

"For God so loved the world that He gave His only begotten Son that whosoever believeth in Him should not perish but have everlasting life" (John 3:16).

Think about it; receiving Jesus as Lord gave you eternal life. This was impossible under the old covenant, but Jesus was the mediator of a better covenant which was ESTABLISHED upon better promises (Heb. 8:6). Under the old covenant, remembrance of sins and sacrifices were made every year, but Jesus made one offering that **"perfected forever them that are sanctified" (Heb. 10:14).**

"By His own blood, He (Jesus) entered in once into the holy place, having obtained eternal redemption for us" (Heb. 10:12). Can you grasp this liberating truth? You are eternally saved with everlasting life . . . The covenant of salvation is forever, Calvary never has to be repeated, the work is done resulting in ETERNAL REDEMPTION – is not that wonderful? If that doesn't put security in your heart, then nothing else will.

Jesus offered Himself through the ETERNAL Spirit without spot to God, thus giving us the promise of ETERNAL INHERITANCE (Heb. 10:10-14).

Saved by His grace divine,

Saved by His power divine,

Life now is sweet

And my joy is complete

For I'm saved, saved, saved!

The Boldness Of Righteousness

There is nothing like right-standing with God to build your confidence and your strength. To know that God has made you the RIGHTEOUSNESS OF GOD in Christ delivers a great sigh of relief to the child of God. It means the struggle is over and that Jesus won the battle for you. God has pronounced you righteous and there is nothing the devil can do about it!

No longer is condemnation sharing the day with you. No longer are negative thoughts harassing you and stealing your joy. You are walking in knowledge of the new person God has made you. Since Christ came in, you are a "new man" or a new creation. What does the Word say? **"Put on the new man which after God is <u>created in righteousness</u> and true holiness" (Eph. 4:24).**

Bold As a Lion

Two quotations from the book of Proverbs: **"The <u>righteous</u> are <u>bold as a lion</u> . . . a lion which is strongest among beasts, and turneth not away for any" (Prov. 28:1, 30:30).** Some view the children of God as a bunch of weaklings but that is not the picture the Word of God portrays. When the early church were baptized in the Holy Ghost, **"they spake the Word of God with boldness" (Acts 4:31).**

Righteousness came to the forefront; it didn't take a backseat to anyone. The believer's position of righteousness enables him to be bold when our adversary, the devil, gets in the way. The Apostle Paul spoke of **"putting on the breastplate of righteousness"** as part of the believer's spiritual armor **(Eph. 6:10-19).** In the Apostle Paul's letter to Timothy, he admonished Timothy not to be hindered by the spirit of fear. Fear is a troubling emotion that torments those who are not mature in the love of God.

Our family had moved across town into a different house. During the first night when we were all bedded down, my young son called out to me and said, "Daddy, I'm scared!" I responded by saying, "It's all well, David. Mommy and Daddy are right here and Jesus is with us." I remember him saying, "All right, Daddy!" At that moment, hearing his Dad's voice and his comforting words released him from fear. Love overcomes fear and the torment it has.

"God hath not given us the spirit of fear, but of power, and of love, and of a sound mind"

2 Tim. 1:7

Paul instructed Timothy, **"God hath not given us the spirit of fear, but of power, and of love, and of a sound mind" (2 Tim. 1:7).** Child of God, see yourself "IN CHRIST;" it will cure your weakness, fear, and inabilities. View yourself a "NEW CREATION" with LOVE, POWER, and with a SOUND MIND. Put on the full armor of God and walk each day in the knowledge of the NEW MAN OF RIGHTEOUSNESS.

God-Given Boldness to Come into His Presence

Every believer is invited to come boldly before God without timidity. **"For now in Christ Jesus ye who sometimes were far off are made nigh by the blood of Christ. For He is our peace, who hath . . . broken down the middle wall of partition between us (Eph. 2:13).**

"Having therefore, brethren, <u>boldness</u> to enter into the holiest by the blood of Jesus . . . Let us draw near with a true heart <u>in full assurance of faith</u>, having our hearts sprinkled from an evil conscience, and our bodies washed with pure water" (Heb. 10:19, 22). What a wonderful Savior, High Priest, and Lord we have over the household of faith.

The Throne of Mercy and Grace

Notice these following words depicting the throne of our Heavenly Father. **"We have not an high priest which cannot be touched with the feelings of our infirmities (frailties, weaknesses, sicknesses, diseases) but was in all points tempted (tried) like as we are, yet without sin. Let us therefore <u>come boldly</u> unto the throne of <u>grace</u>, that we may obtain <u>mercy</u> and find <u>grace</u> (favor) to help in time of need" (Heb. 4:15-16).** Notice that His throne is a throne of GRACE, where MERCY is found. It is a place where those who come will find COMPASSION and HELP for their every infirmity.

The invitation is given twenty-four hours a day to come to the throne of grace. Isn't that wonderful? The sinless blood of Jesus was shed on our behalf enabling us to come into His presence washed and cleansed from every sin and to stand in His righteousness.

Many have a wrong understanding and concept of the believer's right to stand before God. They believe that it is a time to be intimidated, shame-faced, unworthy, and afraid.

But every child of God can now draw near with a true heart in full assurance of faith.

The Veil Was Rent

When Jesus on the cross gave up His spirit to God, He cried, **"It is finished" (John 19:30).** The Bible records a dramatic moment in history. The Temple veil was rent (torn, ripped) from top to bottom. No longer was man shut out of the Holy of Holies. He could now gain access into the presence of the Living God through the finished work of Calvary. **"Jesus, when He had cried again with a loud voice, yielded up the ghost. And, behold, the veil of the Temple was <u>rent</u> in twain from top to bottom; and the earth did quake, and the rocks rent; and the graves were opened; and many bodies of the saints which slept arose" (Mt. 27:50-52).**

What a wonderful witness we have here to the world. We don't hear much about it but every believer needs to sit up and take notice of this climactic event. Heaven did not let it go unnoticed; even the rocks on the earth were split asunder. The graves opened up and the sleeping saints stirred in their graves and were resurrected. Hallelujah! Heaven was not going to let this happen without a spectacular manifestation of God's power.

How wonderful is it that we the redeemed have been given, through the precious blood, the right to come BOLDLY to the Throne of our God. It cost Jesus everything to make it all possible, but He did it.

> I'll praise His Name forevermore
> I'll praise His Name forevermore
> I'll praise, and praise, and praise, and praise!
> I'll praise His Name forevermore!

THE WONDER-WORKING POWER OF THE BLOOD OF JESUS

What can wash away my sin? Nothing but the blood of Jesus.

What can make me whole again? Nothing but the blood of Jesus!

> His blood reaches to the highest mountain
> It flows to the lowest valley.
> The blood that gives me strength from day to day,
> It will never, never, never lose its power.

> There is a fountain filled with blood
> Drawn from Emmanuel's veins,
> And sinners plunged beneath that flood
> Lose ALL THEIR GUILTY STAINS!

We keep hearing that a cashless society is coming and it seems to get closer every day. It is said that currency will be a thing of the past! Many today are also developing a bloodless salvation. It is called the "New Enlightenment." People today are being swept away into this new emerging church as it is referred to. It doesn't regard Jesus, let alone His redeeming blood to wash away sin. The Word of God declares that **"without the shedding of blood, there is no remission (blotting out) of sin (Heb. 9:22).**

The Bible says, **"They have gone the way of Cain" (Jude 11).** Cain was an interesting character. He was the older brother of Abel. When bringing an offering to God, Cain brought the work of his own hands, being fruits and vegetables from the earth. But his brother brought a lamb from the flock which God accepted. Cain became very belligerent as God had no respect for his offering. This made Cain mad and eventually he murdered his righteous brother, Abel (Gen. 4:1-8).

You see Cain was forming his own religion which was the works of his own hands. It came from the earth but Abel's offering was of a heavenly nature. Abel's offering was a type of Jesus, the Lamb that was slain. God accepts nothing else than the sacrifice of His Son and the blood He shed. Other earthly, man-made methods are not acceptable to God. They are a deviation from divine truth that cannot save, heal, or deliver.

The blood of Jesus is God's only cleansing stream that cleanses mankind from sin and unrighteousness. The Bible says, **"Ye were not redeemed with corruptible things, as silver and gold, . . . but with the precious blood of Christ, as a lamb without blemish and without spot" (1 Peter 1:18-19).** In this world, it takes money to redeem something, but when it comes to our soul, it can only be bought back with the sinless blood of Jesus. There was nothing more valuable and precious than the life of God's Son.

We Must Come Under the Blood

> I am the Lord . . . and when I see the blood, I will pass over you"
>
> Exodus 12:13

Back in the days of Egypt when the Israelites were held in slavery, a powerful thing happened. Every dwelling belonging to the Israelites was required by God to be sprinkled with the blood of a lamb. The blood of the lamb was applied to the door.

Here is what God said, **"I will pass through the land of Egypt this night, and will smite all the firstborn in the land of Egypt, both man and beast . . . I will execute judgment, I AM THE LORD. And the blood shall be to you for a token upon the houses where ye are, and when I see the blood, I will**

pass over you" (Exod.12:12-13).

It is a Jewish Biblical custom today to celebrate the Feast of Passover. It is more than interesting that Jesus was crucified at the time of the Passover, as Jesus is our Passover Lamb that was slain for the sins of the world. A type and shadow of Calvary was portrayed in Egypt. The Hebrew people were sheltered and covered within their dwellings, but not so for the Egyptians. The Bible declared that there was a great cry at midnight throughout Egypt as the judgment of God was poured out. It is time for us to come under the covenant of the blood of Jesus where death has no power over us, where sickness and disease cannot reign, and our enemies are defeated!

We Are Made Righteous Through the Blood

Our righteous position is secured by His blood. **"And to Jesus, the mediator of the new covenant, and to the blood of sprinkling, that speaketh better things than that of Abel" (Heb. 12:24).** There are certain things in this life that continue to speak to us. For example a memorial speaks of men going to war. The space shuttle Endeavor, now on exhibit in Los Angeles, continues to speak to us about space exploration. If it is still there in 100 years, it will still be speaking. The blood of Jesus speaks of redemption, forgiveness, sanctification, righteousness, and deliverance. It is speaking on our behalf and it never ceases. When you first applied the blood of Jesus to your life, it began a permanent, on-going process of cleansing. You came under its covering and it is speaking on your behalf every moment of every day.

His blood is not just speaking for you intermittently. No, you are an ongoing partaker of His blood covenant. His blood is not just atoning for you when you feel like it is. You are a blood-bought, already purchased child of God. Jesus has been **"made unto you wisdom, righteousness, sanctification, and redemption" (1 Cor. 1:30).**

Aren't you happy that you are covered by His blood right now as you are reading this book? You will wake up tomorrow morning still under His blood. Believers who walk in the power of the blood are at peace with God and with themselves as their faith is in the continual covering of the blood. When we came to Christ, confession was made for our sin and unrighteousness. We confessed our sins to God and believed for His forgiveness. Here's what the Word reveals, **"If we confess our sins, He is faithful and just to forgive us our sins, and <u>to cleanse us from all unrighteousness</u>" (1 John 1:9).**

Now the conclusion we must arrive at is, that if God says, He has cleansed us from <u>ALL</u> unrighteousness (and "all" means simply <u>everything</u>), then we must be righteous. We have fellowship with God, nothing stands between us and our Heavenly Father. His blood has effectively cleansed us from ALL unrighteousness.

Why is it that so many Christians are sin-conscious instead of being righteousness-conscious? If God says we are righteous, then we can agree with God! May God give us the grace to accept the miraculous work of New Creation because that is who we are when we are in Christ. Jesus said, **"I judge no man (after the flesh)" (John 8:15)** and Paul later stated **"Therefore if any man be IN <u>Christ</u>, he is a <u>new creature</u>: old things are passed away, behold, all things are become new" (2 Cor. 5:17).**

There Is Therefore Now No Condemnation

That statement is almost too good to be true, yet it is true! Here's what the Word of God says, **"There is therefore now no condemnation to them which are in Christ Jesus" (Rom. 8:1).** Are you one of them? Are you in Christ? Then God has made you a NEW CREATION. You are a new kind of person recreated in Christ Jesus unto good works (Eph. 2:10).

> **"There is therefore now no condem-nation to them which are in Christ Jesus"** Rom. 8:1

Condemnation has absolutely no place in the believer's walk with God. Condemnation is a death sentence. Jesus said, **"Verily, verily, I say unto you, he that heareth My Word and believeth on Him that sent Me <u>hath everlasting life</u> and <u>shall not come into condemnation</u>, but is <u>passed from death unto life</u>" (John 15:24).** He also said, **"God sent not His Son into the world to condemn the world, but that the world through Him might be saved" (John 3:17).** God is in the saving business, not the condemning business. God pities His children and He is compassionate toward them. Condem-nation has no mercy on its victims.

When condemnation comes knocking on your door, the best thing to do is to let Jesus answer the door. Condemnation is a weapon the enemy hurls at the children of God, to cripple them and rob them of their joy and victory they have in Christ Jesus.

Condemnation has dreadful effects on a person. It backs them into a corner of depression, self-rejection and worthlessness. If that isn't the work of the adversary then we must ask ourselves the question, "What is?" Self-condemnation makes people physically sick; it has adverse effects all around on every life it claims.

Child of God, never take the put-downs of the enemy. Stand your ground. God's love for you is far greater than any kind of failure the enemy may accuse you of. The Bible makes it clear: he, the devil, is the accuser of the brethren (Rev. 12:10). The enemy is the believer's plaintiff. He brings accusations against you, he wants to get something on you, maybe some things of your past, things you did or didn't do, or some unfortunate circumstance. The enemy is an accuser of the brethren!

None of this alters God's agape, unchanging love for you. Your position of <u>righteousness</u> is unalterable and God's abounding grace still has you covered. Next time the enemy subtly sidles up to you, send him on his way and tell him to take it up with Jesus!

The Work of Righteousness

My friend, when we open our heart to the gift of His righteousness, it will have a heavenly effect upon our lives. You see, righteousness is from Heaven – it comes from above. Good friends of mine used to sing that song, "Heaven Came Down and Glory Filled My Soul." In a world of trouble and strife, Heaven can flood our souls with its glory.

Isaiah explained the working of His righteousness. **"The work of righteousness shall be <u>peace</u>; and the effect of righteousness <u>quietness</u> and <u>assurance</u> forever. And My people shall dwell in a peaceable habitation, and in sure dwellings, and in quiet resting places"** **(Is. 32:17-18).**

The Psalmist David stated, **"He leadeth me in the paths of righteousness" (Ps. 23:3).** The path of righteousness is a path of GOODNESS, PEACE, JOY, LOVE, REST, and BLESSED QUIETNESS. Can you get a glimpse of your glorious position of righteousness? God has filled us with the fruits of righteousness. Isaiah also said, **". . . and righteousness (shall) remain in the fruitful field"** **(Is. 32:16b).**

Why should the believer always be thinking of sin? Why should sin and its nature always be occupying our thoughts? It's like seeing the hole but not the donut! Our prayer should not be, "Lord, please keep me from sin," but rather, "Lord, let Your righteousness reign in my life today!"

I heard of a man who had a problem with drinking. One day while passing by the tavern, he began to get tempted, so he said to the devil, "Get behind me, Satan!" So he did, and pushed him right through the door!

If the enemy can keep a believer focused on sin and failure, then he has him defeated. You can't drive a car looking through the rear view mirror. When the believer's focus and attention is on Jesus and Him alone, he doesn't wander, sink, or fall.

Having Our Mind Set

When God has our thoughts that's when He has us. It was when the disciple Peter took his eyes off of the Master, he began to sink and be afraid. Yet just as soon as he looked to Jesus again, Jesus reached out and saved him. Many are sinking today in the sea of despair; they are trying to do it on their own when life without Jesus becomes very hard. Peter's story had a joyous ending, and ours can too!

Perfect Peace

You will be kept in PERFECT PEACE when your mind is stayed (set) on Him (Jesus) because you trust in Him. Trust in the Lord forever, for in the Lord JEHOVAH (our provider) is everlasting strength **(Is. 26:3-4)**.

Chapter Four

FREEDOM FROM GUILT

The church we pastored for ten years in Idaho Falls, Idaho had a large lit-up marquee in front which at the time read **"Freedom From Guilt."** The church was situated on a major boulevard and it caught the eyes of scores of people.

> **"They shall know the truth and the truth shall set them free"**
> **John 8:32**

A married couple happened to be driving by and noticed the sign, "Freedom From Guilt." It so moved them that the wife decided to attend the service that Sunday morning. They were members of a Mormon ward in our town but trouble had struck their relationship and they were desperate and crying out for help.

I noticed the woman and saw her weeping throughout the service as the Holy Spirit was speaking to her. She responded to the altar call, and Jesus touched her and delivered her from the heavy burden that was weighing her down. Isn't that just like Jesus? Like the woman of Samaria, she returned for the evening service with her husband and their six children. Jesus got a hold of them all, and talk about the joy of the Lord -- it flowed like a river and it got all over the church!

THE ANNOINTING DESTROYS THE YOKE

God often works like that; one gets it that all may get it. Praise God for the anointing of the Holy Spirit. The Word informs us that the anointing destroys the yoke **(Is. 10:27).** It is the anointing that we need today, the precious anointing of the Holy Spirit. Nothing can stand up to a church that is anointed and filled with the Holy Spirit.

"We are called not to deliver sermons, but to deliver the people."

The anointing was the key to Jesus' ministry, for the Word tells us, **"How God anointed Jesus of Nazareth with the Holy Ghost and with power, who went about doing good, and HEALING ALL THAT WERE OPPRESSED BY THE DEVIL . . ."** (Acts 10:38).

I must finish the story. This family left the dead church they were in and they never missed a meeting. Every time the doors were open, they were there. Eventually, they moved out of state. Our church prayed over them and sent them on their way, full of God's blessing. Jesus said, **"They shall know the truth and the truth shall set them free" (John 8:32).**

THE HEAVY BURDEN OF GUILT

Guilt is a heavy burden to bear. It means "to cut off," to be "desolate," and to be "punished." It also implies "to be under or beneath." Guilt is living under a sentence. You may think, "What a dreadful way to live!" Yet sadly, life's pathway is met with many under the load of guilt.

God's Word states **"All have sinned, and fall short of the glory of God" (Rom. 3:23)** and further, **"There is none righteous, no, not one" (Rom. 3:10).** That is our state before we kneel at the cross and come to Christ. At that precise moment, a miraculous transformation occurs and we are made NEW CREATURES in Christ. In an instant, in the twinkling of an eye, Jesus turns our darkness into light. He is still turning the water into wine. **"Old things are passed away; behold, all things are become new" (1 Cor. 5:17).**

Delivered From the Curse

The Word of God declares that Jesus has DELIVERED us from the curse, the punishment of the Law. Jesus took our blame to the cross of Calvary and our blame was put on Him. That being the case, the devil's blame game is over! Jesus settled it at the cross. Now we are living in the blessing of His finished work. Amen!

Can you see it, child of God? No longer can the enemy charge you with anything. The charges against you have been dropped. The case is closed! You walk away a free man or a free woman. The next time the enemy tries to lay something on you, tell him to take it up with Jesus. When he comes knocking, let Jesus answer the door. He won't like that one bit!

You see, guilt has no place in the believer's life. Jesus has cleared your name and forgiven you of all your wrong doings. Praise Him for the blood that soaked deep into your soul and washed you whiter than snow.

HE HEALED US

"By His stripes we are healed" (Is. 53:5).

Calvary made us whole from the crown of our heads to the soles of our feet. When was the last time you affirmed that? I believe it will run the devil off so fast, faster than you can say, "Praise the Lord." Not enough folk declare what He has done for them. Confession brings possession!

Recently, I was endeavoring to help a downhearted young mother. It seemed that she just wasn't coping with her young toddler. She said, "I just feel like giving up all the time." I am sure the enemy is behind circumstances like this. He moves in to disrupt wherever he has an opening. It is not the will of God for you to put yourself down and to think such demeaning things about yourself – that's NOT God! If the enemy can get you to feel badly about yourself, he has won a major victory. The Word tells us to **"Give (no) place to the devil" Eph. 4:27).** That means to give him no advantage over you.

The enemy will have us spinning in circles if we allow him to. "You should have done better!" "If only I had . . ." "If only I had listened, it wouldn't have turned out this way." Life has many of these. They can be breeding grounds for guilt, or stepping stones to higher ground. Give God your disappointments, failures, and mistakes, and move on. Don't dwell on the "whys." They can prevent God's grace and favor from reigning in your life.

> **"I know the thoughts that I think toward you, saith the Lord, thoughts of peace, and not of evil, to give you a future and a hope"**
>
> **Jer. 29:11**

I may not know you, my friend, and may not have even met you, but I know what God says about you. Listen to His words, **"I know the thoughts that I think toward you, saith the Lord, thoughts of peace, and not of evil, to give you a future and a hope"** (Jer. 29:11).

We must refuse the enemy the opportunity to back us into a corner and to browbeat us with guilt. He has no right to accuse you as the Lord has stripped him of that right. When Ruth lay at the feet of Boaz, her nearest kinsman, he extended the border of his skirt over her. In other words, he covered her with his own garment. She encountered GRACE and ACCEPTANCE. He could have rejected her, but unfeigned love and kindness moved him to embrace her **(Ruth 3:8-11; 4:9-10).**

When God told you He loved you, it wasn't for a day but for time and eternity. Nothing can alter it or change His mind. His mind is made up about you – that's just the way it is!

Chapter Five

FAITH: YOUR INWARD CERTAINTY

We were moving to a new town and that afternoon we were to set out looking for a house. Some folks had invited us to lunch and when we parted, the last thing our host said was, "Well, good luck!" I said to myself, "Good luck . . . what's that have to do with it?"

The statement, "Good luck" in my mind was a misquote, it just didn't connect. It was like, "I hope you get lucky and luck is on your side; if not, try again!" I wanted to say, "We're looking for a place to live, not going to Las Vegas!"

I don't know about you but I shrink when I hear that word "luck!" It goes against all we have ever learned concerning placing our faith in the living Word of God. God hasn't called us to live by luck or chance, but by faith.

> **"This is the confidence that we have in Him, that if we ask <u>anything</u> according to His will, He heareth us. And if we know that He hears us, whatsoever we ask, we know that we have the petitions that we desired of Him"**
> **1 John 5:14-15**

What specific statements we have here, like: "<u>the</u> **confidence** <u>that we have in Him</u>," "<u>ask anything</u>," "<u>we know that He hears us</u>," and "<u>we have the (things) we ask (desire) of Him</u>."

Faith is a knowing that **"My God shall supply all your need according to His riches in glory by Christ Jesus" (Phil. 4:19).** Faith is having confidence that He is the guarantee of His faithfulness.

The word "FAITH" is a word seldom used in our modern world as the word "faith" is usually used in a spiritual sense. It is found around 250 times in Scripture. It comes from the Greek word, *"pistis."* Various words in English are used to describe its meaning including the following: "inward certainty," to "agree," to "trust," have "confidence," "evidence," "believe," "reliance on Christ," "faithfulness of God," and "confess."

I want you to know that it was not luck that prevailed in us finding the right house, but FAITH! God spoke to me about a certain man in the town – to ask him if he would rent his house. He was startled for a minute, but said he would. It turned out to be a blessing from God.

It has been that way throughout our years of ministry. God has never failed but has always come through. We're not living by luck or happenstance. We serve a living God who is forever ordering our steps and is mindful of our every need.

AGREEING WITH GOD

Every believer has the right to this miracle-working faith. It is not just for a select few. God is no respecter of persons. You have a right to His **"exceeding great and precious promises" (2 Peter 1:4)** found in God's Word.

When a believer takes a promise from God's Word and wraps it in believing faith, it sets the pace for a miracle. God loves to be reminded of His Word. One of the meanings of "faith" is "to confess", "to say the same thing." Faith is simply agreeing with God.

God loves it when you agree with Him – when you are on the same page with Him and in agreement with His Word. It releases the power of God into the circumstances. Agreement with God is believing His Word cannot fail.

The Documented Word

When Jesus was tempted by the devil, Jesus answered him by saying, **"It is written."** In other words, He referred the devil to the documented Word of God, the holy writ. The devil did not like that, not one bit! When the devil comes up against the Word of God, he bolts for his life. Jesus, each time, stuck to His guns and defeated him **(Luke 4:6-13).** The Word of God in the believer's mouth is also very quick and powerful. The devil does not want to mess with the truth.

A friend of mine bought a lottery ticket. In a few days, he ran it by the scanner which read, "Not a winner." It could have read "LOSER." I told him he should have invested that dollar in the Kingdom of God as God has no losers! He doesn't work on a "good luck" system. His Word does not return void. God's return program is backed up by the bank of Heaven, and it has no losers, only winners! Hallelujah!

The Power of Your Faith

Faith is the very life blood of the Kingdom of God. It is how it works! **"For without faith, it is impossible to please God (Heb. 11:6).** Nothing works in the Kingdom of God without faith. But on the other hand, **"He is a rewarder of those who diligently seek Him (Heb. 11:6).** Jesus always responded favorably to those who reached out in faith. His words to them were, **"Your faith has made you whole" (Mt. 9:22).** It is easy to sit back in the boat of safety, but it takes courage to step out on the waters of faith and trust God to meet your need.

When Paul and Barnabas were in Galatia, in the city of Lystra, they witnessed the power of God.

> **There sat a certain man at Lystra, impotent is his feet, being a cripple from his mother's womb, who had never walked. The same heard Paul speak, who steadfastly beholding him and perceiving that he had faith to be healed, said with a loud voice, Stand upright on thy feet! And he leaped and walked (Acts 14:7-10).**

> **"Faith comes by hearing, and hearing by the Word of God"**
>
> **Rom. 10:17**

The incredible spirit of FAITH came alive as Paul preached the anointed Word of God. The Word of God tells us that **"Faith comes by hearing, and hearing by the Word of God" (Rom. 10:17).** When the Holy Spirit bears witness to the Word of God, then BAM! Faith explodes and miracles begin to take place. God is searching for faith in the hearts of people.

There was a little boy who misquoted his memory verse, "I will not leave you comfortable." Paul wrote to Timothy and said, **"Stir up the gift of God which is in thee" (2 Tim. 1:6).** The word "stir" denotes stirring a fire. The fire of faith needs to burn in our hearts if we desire to see the power of God. You can see the power of God in your life if you so desire. Put a demand on your faith. Let God stretch you and enlarge your capacity of faith. The Word tells us, **"God hath dealt to every man the measure of faith" (Rom. 12:3).** The disciples said to Jesus, **"Increase our faith" (Luke 17:5).** God will take us from faith to faith, from victory to victory, from glory to glory, and from mountain top to mountain top.

God would have us take bigger steps and believe Him for bigger things. I heard of an elephant being tied up with a short rope. He stayed there all day long. He was conditioned to his limitation and he accepted it.

Let these words of Isaiah speak to you: **"Enlarge the place of thy tent, and let them stretch forth the curtains of thine habitations; spare not; lengthen thy cords, and strengthen thy stakes. For thou shalt break forth (expand) on the right hand and on the left"** (Is. 54:3, 4).

Your Faith Grows Exceedingly

Paul wrote to the Thessalonians and said, **"Your faith groweth exceedingly" (2 Thess. 1:3)** How would you like that on your report card? People are watching you! Brothers/sisters, your faith is giving glory and praise to God. Your faith is giving off vibrations and signals that Jesus is alive and at work in you. Amen!

Faith is not to be shut up within the four walls of the church. Faith is for the marketplace, the office, and the battlefield. It may need wisdom and discretion, yet praise God, it is there! Again, the faith of God is in you! Doesn't that make you happy? Faith is where the rubber meets the road.

It just comes down to the fact that faith works! It is undaunted, it won't be silent, it won't take "no" for an answer, and it doesn't withhold.

Speaking the Word of Faith

Friend, believing faith always has a confession and faith always has a "good report." When the twelve spies returned from spying out the land, ten of the spies had an evil report **(Num. 13:32)** but the other two, Joshua and Caleb had a good report. These two said, **"Let us go up at once and take possession, for we are well able to overcome it" (Num. 13:30).** The ten unbelieving spies saw only how it could not be done and spread their unbelief and doubt among the people. The entire nation of Israel had to keep wandering around the wilderness for forty long years because of their unbelief. God said it could be done; they thought they knew better and disagreed with God.

When Israel finally went in and possessed the land, God gave Joshua specific commands; they were to follow instructions and speak only the Word of the Lord. It **"shall not depart out of thy mouth" (Josh. 1:8).** In other words, they were all to speak the same thing. The tongue can either do us good or do us bad; it can be a tree of life or it can ensnare us.

FAITH IS ALIVE

> **"God calleth those things which be not as though they were"**
>
> **Rom. 4:17**

It may seem odd to say that righteousness speaks or that it has a voice, but so does faith. At times, faith speaks loud and clear within the believer's spirit. If you noticed, our main verse spoke of the **spirit of faith.** This would indicate that faith is alive. Just as a person can have a "spirit of fear," so we can have a spirit of faith. **"God . . . calleth those things which be not as though they were" (Rom. 4:17).**

During an early morning prayer meeting at our church in Idaho Falls, Idaho, I felt led to share with the group that we needed a wood-burning stove for the entry meeting area. It was winter and very cold. Everyone saw the need and began to praise God for this stove. A young lady went to where she thought it would go and pretended to warm her hands. I asked her what she was doing and she replied, "I am warming my hands at the stove." Well, it caught on and we all did the same thing, warming ourselves by a fire that wasn't there. I must tell you, in a miraculous way, a man heard about it and gave the church a large stove he had stored in his garage. By Sunday morning, the stove was installed with a hearth and a chimney,. The people were warming themselves, just like we had prayed.

A Word-based believing prayer can have amazing results. **"This is the confidence that we have in Him, that if we ask <u>anything</u> according to His will, He hears us. And if we know that He hears us, whatsoever we ask, we know that we have the petitions that we desired of Him" (1 John 5:14-15).**

Faith Takes a Stand

When we send out the Word, speaking it in faith, we are speaking life. We need to take a stand in the face of opposition and to say, "No, that's not how it's going to be." In Job, we read, **"You will also decree a thing, and it shall be established unto thee; and the Lord shall shine upon thy ways" (Job 22:28).** WE NEED TO SERVE SENTENCE ON THE ENEMY and put him to flight in Jesus' Name. David took a stand when Goliath of Gath defied the armies of the living God. Although he was young in age, yet he was mature in faith. David took a stand and that day, Goliath met his match as David took him out!

Here is your declaration, **"No weapon that is formed against thee shall prosper" (Is. 54:17).** Too many of God's people take their challenges lying down; they let their enemy back them into a corner. The Word tells us, **"having done all, to stand" (Eph. 6:13).** Take your victory; it is yours! Tell the enemy he is trespassing on God's property and you won't stand for it. The Apostle James says, **"Resist the devil and he will flee from you (James 4:7).** He can only take what you give him. Give him nothing! The Word makes it clear, **". . . nor give place to the devil" (Eph. 4:27).** In simple translation: run him off, head him off at the pass!

Jesus said to His followers, **"Behold, I give you the power (authority) . . . over all the power of the enemy" (Luke 10:19).** That power and authority is in the Name of Jesus. It is also in the breastplate of righteousness. In other words, you are standing in oneness with Jesus, the Head of all principalities and powers. You have His will, you have His Word, and you have His Name. What more do we need to defeat our adversary, the devil? **"In all these things, we are more than conquerors through Him that loved us" (Rom. 8:37).** Isn't that wonderful?

Faith – Your Overcoming Power

What does the Lord say? **"Whatsoever is born of God overcometh the world. And this is the victory that overcometh the world – even our faith" (1 John 5:4).** Every believer is born of God. Confessing Jesus Christ as Lord of your life places you on the winning side of life. It makes you more than a conqueror through Him. Isn't that simply wonderful? You see, the Greater One has come to dwell in you. Hallelujah! **"Greater is He that is in you than he that is in the world" (1 John 4:4).**

The Apostle Paul placed high value on his faith. He said, **"I live by the faith of the Son of God, who loved me, and gave Himself for me" (Gal. 2:20).** Notice he declared, "I live by (it)." In other words, I would die without it. I wouldn't survive without the faith of God.

Faith is the believer's greatest asset; lose it and you slide into the ordinary mode instead of the extraordinary. Faith lifts you out of the natural into the supernatural. It takes you from the realm of the impossible into the possible. Faith is the VICTORY that overcomes the world.

What Seemed Impossible

I wanted to fly back to the United States out of Sydney, Australia and they said, "We cannot get you onto this flight,

Mr. Marsh. This is what you will have to do. . . " At that moment, they returned my luggage from the belt and dropped it beside me. It looked impossible! I then said to those in charge, "I will be on this flight." Still they reiterated the same.

I turned away and prayed for God's divine intervention. After praying in the spirit of faith, I heard my name called, and God came through. The seat assignment left me with an empty row which gave me room to stretch out on the 14 hour flight back to Los Angeles. What peace, comfort and assurance we can know when we walk by faith and not by sight.

A friend of mine once said, "I've walked by faith for so long, I wouldn't know how to walk any other way!" Faith is anchored in trust, reliance and confidence in our blessed Heavenly Father. **"He hath said, 'I will never leave thee nor forsake thee.' So that we may boldly say, 'The Lord is my Helper and I will not fear what man shall do to me.'" (Heb. 13:5-6).**

The Tongue of the Learned

> **"For the Word is nigh thee, in thy mouth, and in thy heart, that is, the <u>Word of faith</u> which we preach"**
>
> **Rom. 10:8**

Let me reiterate. <u>He</u> has said, so that <u>we</u> might <u>boldly</u> say. Child of God, let your tongue vibrate with His Word. Let God give you the tongue of the learned. That's what you will have when you speak His Word: the tongue of the learned **(Is.**

50:4). Don't you feel like shouting His praise today? Like standing on the highest mountain and declaring, "Our God reigns!"

I WILL NOT FEAR

Fear is simply the adversary to faith. Too many people are tormented by the emotion of fear. We can function in a spirit of fear or in the spirit of faith. The Word says, **"God has not given us the spirit of fear, but of power, and of love, and of a sound mind" (2 Tim. 1:7).**

The spirit of fear can be conquered when a believer renews (renovates) his or her mind with the thoughts of God. The mind needs to undergo a renewal or transformation if we are going to live in the realms of faith. Wrong thought patterns and vain imaginations need to be cast down and ascendency given to the wonderful promises of God.

My prayer is that you might discover a fresh anointing of the Holy Spirit, "get under the spout where the glory comes out!" The Holy Spirit will flush out every blockage and fill you with the pure love of God. You see, **"Faith worketh by love" (Gal. 5:6),** and here is the clincher, **"Perfect love casts out all fear" (1 John 4:18).**

If you are not baptized in the Holy Spirit, then seek Him for this free gift. It is a total experience of the love of God.

The Apostle Paul instructed us in his letter to the Romans, **"The love of God is shed abroad (poured out) in our hearts by the Holy Spirit who was given to us" (Rom. 5:5).** What an amazing picture we have here illustrating the outpouring of the Holy Spirit. It resembles a watershed dispensing floods of water. Think about it; the Holy Spirit flooding our hearts with His overflowing Heavenly love. (I will be sharing more on this subject).

Faith Makes a Way

Some years ago, I received a letter from V. A. Thampy, President of the New India Church of God, South India. His vision was to have their own boat to reach the thousands of people living in the back waters of South India. There were no roads and these people could be reached only by boat.

When I received the letter, the Spirit of the Lord came upon me and I said within myself, "We can do it!" There was a big "Yes" in my spirit. Faith just seemed to "speak" and I could hear it say, "I will give you the plan and all you will need to do is 'ACT' on it."

There is a kind of faith that will overcome every obstacle. It is a faith that casts out doubt and fear. Well, I must tell you, the switch of faith was turned on and God began to work. Within a short time, we had the required $10,000 and we sent it to India. They were able to buy this ferry boat and launch it out into the waterways where thousands and thousands have heard the good news of the Gospel. Churches have been planted everywhere throughout the region.

I have often wondered what we are waiting for. The Word instructs us to **"Cast thy bread upon the waters, for thou shalt find it after many days. Give a portion (serving) to seven and also to eight" (Eccl. 11:1, 2).** We can sit back and see only the mountain or we can begin speaking to it.

> **Jesus said, Have faith in God. For verily, I say unto you, that whosoever shall say to this mountain, "Be thou removed and be thou cast into the sea," and shall not doubt in his heart, but shall believe that those things which he saith shall come to pass, he shall have whatsoever he saith. Therefore, I say unto you, what things**

soever ye desire, when ye pray, believe that ye receive them, and ye shall have them. (Mark 11:22-24).

When Jesus Saw Their Faith

A story in Mark tells us of four men who brought their palsied friend to the Master to be healed. On arrival, they discovered that they couldn't get to Jesus because of the crowd. It was impossible. They ran straight into the mountain! The problem magnified itself so much that it seemed to have no solution, but faith made a way!

Their desire to get this man to Jesus found a way around the situation. We are told that they lowered the sick man down through the roof. They were persistent; they would not be turned away and they would not be denied. The story tells us of the Master's response: **"When he saw their faith,"** **(Mark 2:5),** He healed the man. After getting their miracle, these men went home to their village; they had gotten what they had come for.

Faith in Action

Faith in action is what pleases God. In some cases, it is faith in re-action! God has no pleasure in us when we shrink back or draw back. The problem God had with the Israelites was that they developed **"an evil heart of unbelief" (Heb. 3:12).** It says He became grieved with that generation. They had turned into a generation of "slackers" and began to murmur and drag their feet. It cost them the milk and honey and a home in the Promised Land. There is a heavy price to pay for unbelief. Unbelief goes unrewarded.

Some folks hold on to doubt, fear and unbelief like they are best of friends. Not long ago, I was sharing the same thought with my daughter, Rebecca. I remarked, "These are our enemies and they will do nothing for us except keep us out of the blessing of God." It is important that we take into captivity these hindering spirits and refuse to allow them to have any effect on our lives. David said, **"Let God arise and let His enemies be scattered" (Ps. 68:1).**

Abraham Believed God

Is there a mystical explanation why Abraham is modeled as a man of faith? What was it about him that pleased God? Why was he referred to as a "friend of God?" Perhaps there is no outstanding reason except **"He believed God" (Rom. 4:3).** This means he was obedient to the steps of the Lord. Even the journey he took to Mt. Moriah to offer up his son, Isaac met with persistent and unswerving loyalty to his Heavenly Father. Although the word "love" is not emphasized, what love and commitment was portrayed throughout his life. I would have to say that Abraham loved God with deep simplicity.

Love and Faith

Doesn't the Word make it clear that **"faith works by love" (Gal. 5:6)**? Out of this unbreakable bond of love was born a faith that God couldn't resist. They were friends. Faith and love bring us into friendship with God. **"Abraham believed God and it was accounted unto him for righteousness" (Gal 3:6).**

Abraham gave us the master key to the "Blessing!" The blessing of righteousness came by <u>faith</u>. Right relationship with God is by faith and not by our works. The works we do now are the fruits of His righteousness. The greatest thing we can do is to "believe God." One who has overcome the troubles of life amidst the wilderness of temptation and can still say, "I believe God" has conquered life.

Abraham never wavered. **"He <u>staggered not at the promise of God through unbelief but was strong in faith, giving glory to God.</u> And being fully persuaded that what He had promised, He was able also to**

perform; therefore it was imputed (accounted) to him for <u>righteousness</u>" (Rom. 4:20-22).

God has called us to be people of faith. Nowhere are we told to pray for faith but rather are instructed to "<u>have faith</u>." It is the same with strength; God commands us to "<u>Be strong</u>."

Love is the breeding ground for faith. Faith without love is empty and gives an uncertain sound. The Word says of Jesus, **"When He saw the multitudes, He was <u>moved</u> with compassion" (Mt. 9:36).** It propelled Him into the realm of faith and miracles.

There are hindrances to the workings of faith like <u>doubt</u> and <u>unbelief</u>, <u>fear</u>, <u>unforgiveness</u>, <u>bitterness</u>, and <u>condemnation</u>, just to name a few. These are faith destroyers, faith dampeners, and miracle crushers. But a heart of pure love produces a pure faith.

Are you ready to be baptized in the Holy Spirit? The world is crying out for a people who are immersed in God's love. Faith without <u>love</u> is not enough, and love without faith is incomplete. Together, they are God's perfect measure to see results.

You might be in need of a miracle, my friend. If you are, it is imperative that you begin to act on your faith, for **"faith without works is dead" (James 2:17).** If the realm of faith in your life has been smothered and suppressed, don't feel bad about it; it has happened to us all.

Transcending Love

I would like to return to the thought **"Faith which worketh by love" (Gal. 5:6).** I can't help but believe that our father Abraham worked on the principle of love. From the very moment Abraham heard God's voice, love gripped his soul. He, like the Apostle Paul, became a prisoner of God's love.

Abraham did not love God out of obedience to the Ten Commandments as they had not yet been given. Abraham tasted of God's irresistible love and that was enough for him to abandon himself to the will and purposes of God. Love became his motivation. Love was the engine that drove his faith. It was his springboard into every act of faith and obedience. Abraham "believed God."

TURN ON THE SWITCH OF FAITH

Do something about it. Perhaps the enemy has attacked you and squelched your spirit of faith. You have become oppressed and everything seems overcast and grey. People's lives are overcome with sickness, poverty, fear, and despair. It doesn't have to be there – don't take it lying down. Draw back the curtains and open the windows of your heart. Begin giving God the sacrifice of praise that is the fruit of your lips. Amen! God can give you a breakthrough any time you need it. Turn your switch of faith on – we must give God something to work with!

The lad gave his meager lunch of 2 small fish and some bread to Jesus, and it fed a multitude. The widow of Zarephath baked a cake (loaf) for the man of God with the last of her provisions, and neither the bin of flour nor the jar of oil ran out until the famine in the land was over. The water was turned into wine at the wedding in Cana because those in charge followed Jesus' instructions to fill the water pots with water. The woman who pressed in and touched the hem of Jesus' garment was made whole. Faith is a "doing" word; it demands action and response. Each of these examples shows the action that was taken in order to receive the miracle.

Some folks received a miracle when they planted a seed. I have found that God will meet us where our faith is. Jesus said, **"According to your faith, be it unto you" (Mt. 9:29).** You see, God works by faith; His Kingdom works by faith; and everything you receive, you must take by faith.

I once knew a brother who would constantly say "I receive that!" We only receive what we claim in Jesus' Name. Many believers don't receive because they don't believe they have it. They believe if they see it or can touch it. But what does the Word say? **"Now faith is the substance of things hoped for, the evidence of things not seen" (Heb. 11:1).**

Persistent Faith

There is such a thing as persistent faith. That's the kind that doesn't let up. It keeps knocking and believing. It is a faith that runs deep like a river. It is not like a babbling brook with a lot of noise. Isaiah seems to describe the person with persistent faith. **"In quietness and in confidence shall be your strength" (Is. 30:15).**

Child of God, it is important to cut ourselves off from our traditions, like something we may have heard that doesn't hold an ounce of truth. Our faith must not be based on someone's opinion but rather on the unadulterated Word of God, for God says what He means, and He means what He says.

My family was Baptist in our early years of serving the Lord but later came into the Pentecostal experience which changed our lives. Amen! During those early years we were told that God does not heal today, those days were over, and those things only took place in the early church. Praise the Lord, we found out differently!

"Now faith is the substance of things hoped for, the evidence of things not seen" (Heb. 11:1).

Tradition tried to make the Word of none effect. The first thing my Dad did was to get a big bottle of castor oil and if any of us kids got sick, he would pour on the oil and pray the prayer of faith. Dad's prayers always touched God and we were always blessed and healed through his prayers and the power of God. I can still smell that castor oil today!

Hallelujah! Our God can do anything! He is not a Baptist, Methodist or Presbyterian – He is the Lord, above all, through all, and in us all. We must take the limits off of God and not restrict His power to heal us everywhere we might be hurting.

Turning Your Faith Loose

We might have all the faith in the world yet what good will it do if it stays locked up in our Bible? It must be put into action. What good is a beautiful new car if it is locked up in your garage and never driven? You might have a million dollars in your bank account and never touch a penny of it. Put it to use! The family Bible may have sentimental value yet it just sits on display gathering dust. We are to **"be doers of the Word, and not hearers only" (James 1:22).**

Real faith is to be activated. Faith is not a statue displayed in a cathedral. Faith is alive, and that works out in the real world and in living people like you and me. Your faith can be turned loose on your job. Faith can make you the best salesperson. Faith can make you the best player. Faith works wherever it is exercised. It will work for you if you will turn it loose.

Faith stands upon the Word in all circumstances. Faith says what God says! Faith goes to work when you go to work. Faith gets up out of bed when you do. The faith of God is in you, child of God. It is at your disposal and within your reach. Let it out! Turn it loose and watch things get better and better. You can go to work with unbelief and doubt or you can go to work with the spoken <u>word of faith</u> on your lips.

Jesus said, **"According to your faith so be it unto you" (Mt. 9:29).**

Do you want to enlarge your faith? Then use what you have! You don't need a lot; just use what you've got! Active faith begets (expands) the faith you have. It's like energy and strength; it increases with utilization (use).

A well-meaning lady once said to me, "I believe our faith is personal and private." I thought that sounds respectable but that's not for me. How can the **"SPIRIT OF FAITH"** lay silent and personal? If that is so, then the early church was really out of order. They shouted it from the roof tops and turned their world upside down. They went everywhere proclaiming the good news of the Kingdom.

Friend, I am the first to say that we must exercise wisdom and discretion when it comes to the expression of our faith. Yet at the same time we cannot stand back and be muzzled. There is a world out there needing to hear the good news that Jesus is alive today!

I asked a young man recently, "Would you like me to pray for you?" He answered, "I'd love you to!" Faith can't keep the good things of the Lord to one's self.

> **"Faith is more precious than gold that perishes"**
>
> **I Peter 1:7**

My mother was a classic; she shared Jesus with everyone she met. The bus stop was her mission field as she never did drive a car. I remember her sharing Jesus with children on the beach; she would build three sand castles and share the gospel story. Mother was raised in a religious home with the others never experiencing being born again. But her faith ran very deep into her soul. It was like a river that flowed out from her heart. I thank God she never kept it to herself. That made her days here on earth count for eternity. She won all six of her children to the Lord.

My friend, I believe the Holy Spirit led me to write this book on this wonderful subject of faith – your faith is so vital. The Word tells us, **"Faith is more precious than gold that perishes" (1 Peter 1:7).**

Our gold and silver will perish but our faith in God is eternal and will stand the test of time. Faith is not just a theory or a philosophical belief. Faith is trust in the living God and in our Lord and Savior, Jesus Christ.

Chapter Six

FAITH OR FEELINGS

Have you ever felt like nothing was happening, like things were at a standstill, when all the time, God was at work behind the scenes? In this walk of faith God has called us to, one must learn the difference between our faith and our feelings. I have learned that our feelings can be unreliable and that for positive guidance, we must walk by faith and not by sight.

> **"The just shall live by faith."**
>
> **Rom. 1:17**

There are times in the believer's walk when feelings are at a low ebb, and God seems to be afar off. This is the time to remind ourselves that **"The just shall live by faith" (Rom. 1:17).**

WHY ARE YOU SO FEARFUL?

One time the disciples were on the Sea of Galilee when a storm came up; they were tossed about and afraid for their lives. It so happened that Jesus was there all the time. Besides, Jesus had said at the beginning of the trip, **"Let us pass over unto the other side" (Mark 4:35).** When Jesus spoke this statement, I think He meant every word of it! One way or another, His disciples forgot His words, and fear took the reins of their hearts. After Jesus stilled the tempest and a great calm came over the sea, Jesus addressed their problem by saying, **"WHY ARE YOU SO FEARFUL? How is it that you have no faith?" (Mark. 4:40).**

Friend, God is taking you <u>OVER</u> TO THE OTHER SIDE. Life with its storms and trials may threaten your journey, but

Jesus never fails and He is in the situation with you. We can allow our feelings to fill us with fear or we can grip the firm hand of faith. Most people live in the realm of their feelings. They cannot see beyond their adversity. It consumes them!

Are negative feelings dictating to you how it is going to be, or do you believe God in a true spirit of faith?

NEGATIVE FEELINGS

When you awake tomorrow morning and you feel down even before the day starts, that's the moment to take charge and speak to those feelings of negativity and affirm the Word of faith over your life. Those destructive thoughts will leave you and have no persuasion over you. **God has called us to reign through righteousness!**

Negative feelings take people down the road of defeat, depression, and despair. The enemy (the devil) is behind this way of thinking. Think about it: **God speaks well of us!** People are listening to the wrong voice. There is nothing good about the devil; he is full of mischief and subtlety. Every believer needs to distinguish between the voice of the Holy Spirit and the voice of the enemy.

Jesus never puts us down; He lifts us up with a kind and loving hand. He reaches out to us with tender mercy. The enemy destroys people's lives with his accusations, lies, and deception.

FATHER OF LIES

Child of God, what are you feeling today? Are you feeling that you are a failure, that you are not going to make it? You know, Jesus called the devil the **"father of lies" (John 8:44).** He whispers his lies into the ears of his listeners. It's time to plug our ears to his nonsense and lies, and to BELIEVE THE PROMISES OF GOD. What do you say?

Shut him down! Turn him off! Put a stop to his garbage! Like they say, "Garbage in, garbage out!" Jesus simply rebuked the devil when he spoke out of turn. He silenced him and ordered him to be quiet.

James, in his letter to the churches instructed the saints to **"Resist (stand against) the devil and he will flee from you. Draw close to God and He will draw close to you" (James 4:7-8).**

Knowing Jesus' voice is the secret to the believer's victory. Jesus said, **"(My) sheep . . . know (My) voice. And a stranger will they not follow" (John 10:4-5).** There are many strange voices in the land today leading the people astray, but God the Holy Spirit is speaking too, and leading His people in a plain path; it is called the <u>path of righteousness</u>. Paul said, **"I LIVE BY THE FAITH OF THE SON OF GOD WHO LOVED ME AND GAVE HIMSELF FOR ME" (Gal. 2:20).**

THE FLIGHT OF FAITH

I was flying with other pastors, including my Dad who was visiting the United States at the time, in a twin engine Cessna over the Colorado Rockies heading for my home town of Idaho Falls. It was instrument flying much of the flight as there was no visibility. Our plane was being tossed about and one couldn't help feeling somewhat helpless. The pilot who was the owner of the plane along with a pastor friend had the flight under control as they had complete trust in their instrumentation.

I remember breaking out of the clouds' density and looking over the Snake River valley. It was a magnificent sight to behold. I then thought, "I'm glad the pilots were not flying the aircraft by their feelings through those thick clouds, but rather in the knowledge of their instruments." We had a safe flight and a perfect landing back into Idaho Falls.

Throughout the years, we have learned to trust God on those cloudy days, in those valleys, and in the fight. He carries us through the trials and the hard times only to land us safely on higher ground.

When visibility is zero and you can't see out the windows, FAITH tells you, "HOLD ON AND DON'T LET GO; HE IS TAKING YOU TO THE OTHER SIDE!"

> Feelings come and feelings go,
> Feelings are deceiving.
> My warrant is the Word of God,
> Naught else is worth believing.
>
> Though all my heart should be contemned
> For want of some sweet token,
> There is One greater than my heart
> Whose Word cannot be broken.
>
> I'll trust in His unchanging Word
> Though soul and body sever,
> For though all things shall pass away,
> His Word shall stand forever.

Chapter Seven

GOD'S MIRACLE CURE

In the book of Leviticus 13:44-46, God provides us with a picture of the sin of unrighteousness. Throughout the Word of God, He likens the spiritual to the natural so that we might understand the truth of what God is showing us. Here God reveals to us the corruption of leprosy. Leprosy is a dreaded crippling disease that results in devastation of the human body. This contemptible, loathsome disease leaves a person disfigured, destroyed, and worthless. One cannot describe the pain, suffering, and hopelessness leprosy causes its victims. It is a hellacious condition which abnormally affects the whole person in body, soul, and spirit.

To protect the camp of Israel, extremely strict measures were implemented as leprosy is very contagious. The victim at the outset was branded "unclean" and put out of the camp. He or she wore a mask over their mouth and on approach had to cry out, "Unclean, unclean." Separated utterly from loved ones and from the community, deprived of human dignity, they daily became the off-scouring of the world in which they existed.

INDIA

One time while I was in India, a leprous man stood at my car window, eaten up with this dreaded disease of leprosy. Sitting there, I turned and there he appeared with his fingers gone and face disfigured, begging for a handout. I must tell you, with his face and body only 2 or 3 feet away, I was shocked out of my wits. I still see him to this day after 35 years. What a tragedy befell my eyes that day in Madras, India.

Unspotted

Sin throughout the Word of God resembles leprosy in all of its hideousness. Sin in its various forms is just as destructive and unclean as leprosy. Sin separates us from loved ones, destroys homes, ruins societies, and sends people to hell. Just as a leper lives his life in reproach and shame, so sin takes people down the same road.

The true believer keeps himself from the contamination of sin. He keeps himself "unspotted" from the world. Leprosy doesn't mature overnight. First there are spots that appear, and if left untreated will result in the unmistakable disorder of leprosy.

> **"The wages of sin is death but the <u>gift of God</u> is eternal life through Jesus Christ our Lord"**
> **Rom. 6:23**

Speaking of Jesus, the Word says, **"Thou hast loved righteousness, and hated iniquity" (Heb. 1:8).** The word "hate" is a strong word but that's how it has to be when it comes to iniquity. We are not to tamper with sin any more than we would with leprosy. They both have devastating consequences. **"The wages of sin is death but the <u>gift of God</u> is eternal life through Jesus Christ our Lord" (Rom. 6:23).**

Sin today is playing havoc in our society. Like leprosy, it doesn't discriminate. There is not a city or country town that is not infected. Our beautiful young people are dying each day by the thousands. Our prisons are overcrowded. Society is burdened and hearts are broken.

JESUS' MIRACLE TOUCH

"And it came to pass, when He (Jesus) was in a certain city, behold a man full of leprosy: who seeing Jesus fell on his face, and besought Him, saying, 'Lord, if Thou wilt, Thou canst make me clean'. And He put forth His hand, and touched him, saying, 'I will: be thou clean'. And immediately the leprosy departed from him" (Luke 5:12-13).

In the days of Moses, those infected would be examined by the priest and his present condition would be determined. On this occasion, this man "full of leprosy" came to Jesus, "the Great High Priest" and asked if He would make him clean. Jesus compassionately touched the man and the power of God delivered him from his plague. It took just one touch by the "Great Physician" to restore this man to normalcy. It says, "immediately the leprosy departed from him."

Sin's power is destroyed by the Master's touch. It doesn't matter how deep it is, how bad it is, how shocking; the power of Jesus Christ can deal with it! His blood can make the vilest clean and set the prisoner free. This poor man fell down at the feet of Jesus and this is where we all have to come. We are all sinners and desperate for cleansing, desperate for His forgiveness and renewal. The way up is the way down!

This man, the Bible tells us, was "full of leprosy." Before we come to Jesus, every one of us is full of sin. The Bible makes it clear, **"There is none righteous, no not one" (Rom. 3:10).** Until we fall at His feet, we are full of self-righteousness, pride, and waywardness. As the apostle Paul states, we **"were the servants of sin" (Rom. 6:17).**

Give It All to Jesus

"If we confess our sins, He is faithful and just to forgive us our sins, and to <u>cleanse us from all unrighteousness</u>" (1 John 1:9).

Jesus makes a trade with us. We give Him our old tattered garments; He gives us a robe of pure white. We give Him our mess; He gives us a message! He takes our test; He gives us a testimony! The Psalmist declared, **"He redeemeth (my) life from destruction" (Ps. 103:4a).**

This leper of Jesus' time met with love, mercy, and compassion. He had nothing to give. He had no money, no means of support, only loneliness, rejection, and despair. He not only reached out to Jesus but Jesus reached out to him. The Bible tells us that the religious leaders accused Jesus of being a friend of sinners.

Jesus felt the people's pain. He identified with their hurt. It has been said that two thirds of what is plaguing the multitudes today is the curse of alcohol, substance abuse, pornography, devil worship, and everything that is ungodly. Satan is the destroyer and the deceiver. Jesus said, **"The thief cometh not, but for to steal, and to kill, and to destroy: <u>I am come that they might have life, and that they might have it more abundantly</u>" (John 10:10).**

We must be reminded that **"For this purpose the Son of God was manifested, that He might destroy the works of the devil" (I John 3:8).** Jesus said **"All power is given unto Me in Heaven and in earth" (Mt. 28:18).** No one has ALL POWER but Jesus, the Son of God. Whatever Satan may "dish out," Jesus is greater! Chains of alcohol and drug addiction can be broken. Jesus can open the prison doors to those that are bound. Many sit in darkness and are tormented by fear. They sit in their prison, searching for a way out, wishing things were different and thinking about how things could have been.

It is not until we meet the Man called Jesus that things begin to change! He gave the man full of leprosy a new life, and He will do the same for anyone who will come to Him! Most of Jesus' ministry was taken up with healing the sick, delivering the bound, and setting the captive free.

Nothing could be worse than being a leper; Jesus took the worst case scenario and demonstrated His mercy. This man came to the place where he wanted nothing more than to be healed. His mind was made up and it was now up to Jesus to make it good! To get delivered and set free from the bondage and burden of sin, one must hate his or her present state of being. David said, **"I hate (my enemies) with perfect hatred" (Ps. 139:22).** This is not referring to people but to the enemies of our soul, those soul-destroying, life-destroying hindrances that seek to pull us down.

Believe He Did It

When we ask Jesus to forgive us and to sanctify us, we must believe that He has done it. When we ask Him for something "in Jesus' name," we have it! Jesus said, **"Believe that ye receive them and ye shall have them" (Mark 11:24).** When the Bible states that Jesus took all your sins to Calvary and nailed them to the cross – BELIEVE THAT HE DID IT! We are not to be like a dog that buries his bone and the next day digs it up again. Leave your sins in the sea of God's forgetfulness. Remind yourself that you are a NEW CREATURE in Christ Jesus. Too many believers keep digging up their old bones, but your life is under the blood of Jesus and His blood is declaring you righteous. Amen!

MADE A NEW CREATION

You were once "full of sin" but not anymore. When I was a boy attending a Baptist church, there was a verse of a hymn we sang that went like this, "Vile and full of sin I am!" I know better than to sing that line anymore, particularly since I found out that by God's grace I am the righteousness of God in Christ. I may have been "vile and full of sin" at one time, but not now! I have been made a **"new creation" (2 Cor. 5:17).**

Too many Christians have a wrong confession about themselves. We need to believe who God says we are! His blood has cleansed us from ALL unrighteousness. Why can't I believe that instead of saying, "I'm just a poor old sinner saved by grace?" You can guarantee that leper man who was healed by Jesus did not go around saying, "I'm just a poor old leper saved by grace." That "leper" word was never found in his vocabulary ever again!

It is most important to relate to the new you. We could say that you have an earthly identification and you have a spiritual identification. The Word declares that we **"are partakers of the Heavenly calling" (Heb. 3:1).**

The New Man

What an awesome truth that He has made us new creatures in Christ. We have **"put off"** the **"old man"** and we are to **"put on"** the **"new man"** (Eph. 4:22-24). You might ask. "who is the new man we are to put on?" The NEW MAN is the re-created man, born again of the Spirit of God spoken of in **Eph. 4:24, "created . . . in <u>true righteousness</u>."**

We can also refer to him as the **"inner man" (Eph. 3:16).** Our inner man is the indwelling presence of God; the **"Sun of Righteousness" (Mal. 4:2)** who dwells in the inner sanctuary of our lives. In other words, the believer's body is **"the temple of the Holy Spirit which is in you" (1 Cor. 6:19).** The Bible also refers to the **"outer/outward man" (2 Cor. 4:16)** which is our physical body.

Identification

When God stepped in and revealed His divine purposes to Abraham, we are told that God changed his name from Abram to Abraham. God said, **"Thou shalt be a father of many nations. . . I will make nations of thee, and kings shall come out of thee" (Gen. 17:1-6).** Once Abraham knew this, he had to relate to his heavenly calling. His life took on a new meaning. He was no longer just Abram, a descendant of his earthly father but he had received a higher calling.

> **"He who doeth the will of God abideth forever"**
>
> **I John 2:17**

Christians have a hard time switching over from the earthly to the heavenly. Their heavenly calling is just as real as their earthly calling, except the earthly passes away but **"He who doeth the will of God abideth forever" (1 John 2:17).**

The same thing happened to Sarah, Abraham's wife. **"Thou shalt not call her name Sarai, but Sarah shall her name be. And I will bless her, and she shall be a mother of nations; kings of peoples shall be of her" (Gen. 17:15-16).** This process also occurred with Jacob, their grandson, the son of Isaac. God said, **"'What is thy name?' And he said, 'Jacob.' And He (God) said, 'Thy name shall be called no more Jacob, but Israel: for as a prince hast thou power with God and with men'" (Gen: 32:27-28).**

God has called us out of this world. By this, we have a new identity. Are you holding on to the earthly which has fading value, or are you attentive to His purpose which is eternal?

Isaiah said, **"One shall say, 'I am the Lord's'; and another shall call himself by the name of Jacob; and** another shall . . . surname himself by the name of Israel" (Is. 44:5). There was eagerness within to be adjoined to the Lord and His people. They reveled in the fact that they were partakers of the inheritance of the saints in light. What an outstanding identification the saints have "in Christ." The world jostles with each other, looking for identity and acceptance. It is a train to nowhere, everyone trying to get on board!

Hands Placed Upon the Head

"And thou shalt cause a bullock to be brought to the Lord upon the altar before the tabernacle of the congregation, and Aaron and his sons shall put their hands upon the head of the bullock" (Ex. 29:10).

Under the laws of the Old Covenant, the priests, when offering a sheep or other sacrifice to the Lord upon the altar, would place their hands upon the head of the sacrifice. This had a spiritual significance which speaks of identification. The priests did not just stand back with their arms folded; they became an integral part of the ceremony. The lamb was dying in their stead and in their place. It died vicariously for the sins of the people.

If we want the life-changing power of Calvary to change us, then we of a certainty must lay hold to it. The placing of the priest's hand on the head of the offering meant reaching out and claiming the miracle work for one's self.

Jesus, our sacrificial lamb, died for our sins and He rose again from the dead for our justification. In our weakness and human frailty, we have a place to run to. We have a refuge and a hiding place. Jesus is the rock of our salvation. The Psalmist wrote, **"He shall cover thee with His feathers, and under His wings shalt thou trust" (Ps. 91:4).**

Jesus is our covering. He has you covered, child of God. The big word here is <u>TRUST</u>. Do you trust Him for your covering? Are you relying on His mercy? Have you placed your confidence in His finished work at Calvary?

Feeling Inadequate

> **His love for us does not depend on our goodness**
>
> **but on His unchanging faithfulness.**

When you feel inadequate or incomplete, know that there is One who is complete and lean upon Him. Think of a father who reaches out to his child and draws that one to himself. This is a picture of Jesus. Your shortcomings, misgivings, and complications will never separate you from His love. His love for us does not depend on our goodness but on His unchanging faithfulness. God has never changed His mind about you; you are just as precious to Him today as you were yesterday

My word to you, child of God, is don't linger back in the shadows or hide from His presence. Don't fall away! He is not mad at you. You may be mad at yourself but that doesn't mean that He is. You might be disgusted with who you are, but God has not cast you away like a broken toy or a worn-out rag doll. The Jesus I have come to know over the years never casts us off. People throw people away these days like an unwanted step-child, but not our Heavenly Father. He left the ninety and nine and went searching for the ONE lost sheep. We were all, each one that lost sheep, away from the fold, without God and His Son.

Reach Out

In your need, reach out and place your hand upon "the head" which is Jesus. That way you will be identifying with <u>His</u> righteousness! You never did have any of your own anyway! Reach out to His throne of mercy, to His abounding grace, and He will meet your every need. You are sure to meet Him standing there with His arms outstretched to receive you.

Pronounced Clean

When this poor leper encountered Jesus, the Bible says immediately the leprosy departed. He came "full of sin," and he left a NEW CREATION. Isn't that out of sight? This man met up with Jesus (the High Priest) and he was never the same again. No longer did leprosy reign over him. Jesus can break the grip that sin has over a man's or woman's life and pronounce them clean!

What a wonderful Savior! What a wonderful God! Paul referred to Him (Jesus) as **"(God's) unspeakable gift"** (2 **Cor. 9:15).**

Chapter Eight

JESUS THE HEALER

I was invited to hold some meetings in Fresno, California at Pastor Joseph Thornton's church where I had previously heard of an 18-month-old child in the church who was very sick. Without a miracle, he was not expected to live. For some reason, the Holy Spirit put this child on my heart and I had been seeking the Lord for him. Coming to Fresno for these meetings was in the purpose of God. On arrival, I immediately asked the pastor how the little boy was doing. Brother Thornton explained that the child was in the hospital and that his condition was very grave. Without divine intervention, he would not live. I asked, "Can we go now and pray for him?" Brother Thornton said "Yes," and we went immediately to the hospital.

On arrival and entering the room, I saw a very sick toddler with all kinds of tubes in his head, draining the fluids from his brain. The child was in the last stages of leukemia with only days to live. I knew in my spirit that it was time to go to work and to believe for a miracle for little Forest.

I asked the attending nurse if I could pick up the child and pray for him. She was very cooperative and said, "Yes." For thirty-five minutes I held him close to me, and all I did was speak the Name of Jesus. Tears ran down my cheeks as I interceded for the life of this precious child. It was like I shut myself in with God and became unaware of my surroundings. After thirty-five minutes, I felt the work was done so I placed the child back in his bed and left the hospital. From that day, little Forest began to get well and he miraculously recovered. In a week, they sent him home. In the medical records in Fresno, it stipulates that his cure is unknown.

Today, Forest is about thirty years old and the church is still talking about the miracle. There is wonder working power in the mighty Name of Jesus. All praise is given to Him for this outstanding miracle of His power.

HIS NAME IS AS OINTMENT POURED FORTH

I had a God-fearing mother who thrived on the Name of Jesus. She loved His Name and prayed for us children fervently every chance she got. She believed that all she ever needed was found in His Name. She believed there was salvation and healing in His name. She believed there was safety in His Name. There was protection in His Name. There was victory in His Name. Mother saw every problem resolved in and through His sacred Name. The Name of Jesus released the miracle power of God.

Isaiah spoke of His coming. He declared, **"His Name shall be called <u>Wonderful</u>, <u>Counselor</u>" (Is. 9:6).** Notice the majestic words of the Apostle Paul in his letter to the Philippians:

> **Wherefore God also hath <u>HIGHLY EXALTED</u> Him (Jesus), and given Him a Name which is above every name: that at the name of <u>JESUS</u> every knee should bow, of things in heaven, and things in earth, and things under the earth; and that every tongue should confess that Jesus Christ is Lord. (Phil. 2:9-11).**

Jesus said, **"These signs shall follow them that believe; In My Name shall they <u>cast out devils</u>; they shall speak with new tongues; . . . they shall lay hands on the <u>SICK</u> and they shall recover" (Mark 16:17-18).**

If we silence the Name of Jesus as the devil is doing today, all kinds of problems will plague the people. You see, devils and demons from the kingdom of darkness are rendered powerless where Jesus is exalted. Some great and notable speakers today hardly ever mention the Name of Jesus throughout their sermons. What they seem to say is good, yet is it good enough to deliver our people from the onslaught of the enemy? We praise God for those who are endeavoring to uphold the Word of truth, yet there is a great need for a fresh outpouring of the Holy Ghost and power.

> **"(His) Name is as ointment poured forth."**
> **Song of Solomon 1:3**

Mother's prayer was a session. She prayed fervently as the Spirit led her and pressed in for the answer. The Bible verse Mother used was found in the **Song of Solomon 1:3, "(His) Name is as ointment poured forth."** She would sit by our bed, and with her soft hand stroke our forehead and speak the Name.

When Momma got filled with the Holy Ghost, the Name took on a new meaning. I was very young, yet I saw Mother change from a timid Baptist to a strong woman of faith and power. For Jesus said, **"Ye shall receive power, after that the Holy Ghost is come upon you" (Acts 1:8).**

Oh, how we need the anointing of the Holy Ghost. It is the anointing that destroys the yoke. Our prayers need the power and the authority of the Holy Ghost. Sickness will be driven out and diseases cured in His Name. When Jesus prayed for a young woman, it says He stood over her. Jesus gave the church **"power to tread on serpents" (Luke 10:19)** and to do **"signs and wonders" (Acts 4:30).**

There's victory in His Name; there's power in His Name; there's healing in His Name; and there's deliverance in His

Name. Every believer has been given the power of attorney to use the Name of Jesus. The modern church of today needs to get back to the basics, to the fundamentals of the faith, for His Name is the secret key to the power of God.

Mother would apply the Name of Jesus like she was rubbing in the ointment. I'll tell you it worked in my home and it will work in yours. His Name is as ointment poured forth. Next time you are called to pray for someone, pour it on! Speak His Name with confidence and expect a miracle.

Throughout the Scriptures, ointment is referred to as precious. It says, **"A good name is better than precious ointment" (Eccl. 7:1).** Mary took a pound of spikenard which was very costly and anointed the feet of Jesus. I want to say that no price can be put on the precious Name of Jesus. The Word of God tells us, **"(He is) chosen of God, and precious" (1 Pet. 2:4).** There is a soothing, healing anointing in the awesome Name of Jesus when it is applied in faith to the sick and oppressed. His Name also carries with it authority over all the work of the enemy. Jesus said, **"In My Name shall they cast out devils . . . they shall lay hands on the sick, and they shall recover" (Mark 16:17-18).**

Pour it on the wounded; pour it on the hurting, the bruised, the oppressed, and the bound. Many people are in a world of hurt. Just the mention of His Name is as ointment poured forth. There is a healing balm in Gilead (Gen. 37:25; Jer. 8:22) that makes the wounded whole. Recently, I laid hands on a hurting young man in the Name of Jesus and he began to weep. Yes, His Name is as ointment poured forth. There is SOMETHING ABOUT THAT NAME"

> Precious Name, O how sweet
> Hope of earth and joy of heav'n
> Precious Name, O how sweet
> Hope of earth and joy of heav'n!

PARANOIA OVER THE NAME

The apostles found the master key to God's miracle power. The more they preached in the Name, the more the rulers of the people got mad. Not much has changed today; they are still paranoid about His Name. Buddha is OK, Shinto is OK, Mohammed is OK, but Jesus is too much! Why? Simply because He is the **"King of Kings, and Lord of Lords" (Rev. 19:16)**. **"God hath highly exalted Him and given Him a Name which is above every name, that at the Name of Jesus every knee shall bow" (Phil 2:9-10).** The devil does not like the Name of Jesus; it makes him very uncomfortable. People who hate the Name of Jesus go into self-conscious distress, almost a delirious mode at the mention of His Name. The apostles were warned not to speak in that Name but it still didn't stop them. They took a whippin' but they couldn't be silenced. When the Name is preached, it spreads heaven around and puts the enemy to flight.

Jesus, my friend, can heal you everywhere you hurt. God's word to His people was **"I will restore health unto thee, and I will heal thee of thy wounds, saith the Lord" (Jer. 30:17).** Some people do not pray for the sick. They even believe that God puts sickness on us to teach us something. They believe it is the will of God that they are sick, yet these same people go to the doctor to get better. It seems like they should stay sick so as to be in the will of God!

The Word of God is filled with His promises for the healing of our bodies. The leper came to Jesus and said, **"If thou wilt, thou canst make me clean."** Jesus responded by saying, **"I will, be thou clean" (Mark 1:40-41).** There was nothing to debate. Jesus didn't say "I need to think it over." That diseased man ran clear into the will of God that day and Jesus said "Yes." Some preachers want to get you saved and leave you sick. Sickness is not a work of God.

Sickness needs to be rebuked and sent back to where it came from. Amen!

Let us take a moment and consider the commission of Jesus. **"And when He had called unto Him His twelve disciples, He gave them power against unclean spirits, to cast them out, and to heal all manner of sickness and all manner of disease" (Mt. 10:1).** No one had more compassion than Jesus for the sick and the suffering. They only needed to touch the hem of His garment to be made perfectly whole. He took time for the hurting, the oppressed, and the afflicted. He would cross over the Sea of Galilee, one day's journey, just to deliver one person. Jesus was always about His Father's business, and that was setting the captive free.

> **"How God anointed Jesus of Nazareth with the Holy Ghost and with power, Who went about doing good, and healing all that were oppressed of the devil, for God was with Him"**
>
> **Acts 10:38**

One of the most pronounced references to Jesus healing the sick is found in Acts. Jesus spent a large part of His ministry healing the sick and delivering the bound. Some things are obvious and plain to see what the will of God is. Jesus came to do the will of Him Who sent Him.

The church is now called to do the work of His ministry, for the church is **"His body, the fullness of Him that filleth all in all" (Eph. 1:23).** There are spiritual gifts in the Body of Christ that need to be released to a hurting world. These spiritual gifts are miraculous in nature. They are a divine faculty (gift) of the grace of God. After we are saved, it is essential that we be filled with the Holy Spirit, speaking with a heavenly language.

The Holy Ghost is the gateway to the miraculous. We desperately need His power and anointing if we are to experience the power of God. Some only go so far into the river of His fullness and are satisfied with an ankle-deep experience. The Lord beckons us to come out into the deep, into His fullness. Are you thirsty, child of God, for the fullness of the Spirit? Do you have an unquenchable thirst that just doesn't go away? David said, **"My cup runneth over" (Ps. 23:5).** There's a mighty ministry awaiting the church for these last and final days. There are those who will be called to seek God for a fresh move of the Holy Ghost. Only those who will launch out into the stream of His fullness can know His transforming power.

MIRACLE IN INDIA

Throughout the years of ministry, we have had the opportunity to preach in the land of India. When I was a lad, God visited me in our family home. His Spirit came upon me and He told me I would preach His Word in the land of India. I immediately went to my mother and told her. Well, in an amazing way, it has come to pass. I have lost count of our visits there. We have seen thousands respond to Christ, and thousands healed by the power of God.

After a miracle crusade, a man came to me and asked if I would come to his house and pray for his sister who was completely withdrawn and for two years had not spoken nor left her room. An evil spirit of darkness bound her and took her captive. Brother Thornton happened to be with me on this visit so he went with me. The woman sat motionless on her bed and said nothing. We spoke to that evil spirit and commanded it to come out of her and to never come back. God heard our prayer that day and delivered that tormented woman. Sometime later, her brother wrote me from Canada with a praise report. He explained that his sister came out of it and that she was now married with a child. To God is the glory! Jesus said, **"Ye shall receive power (authority),** after that the Holy Ghost is come upon you" (Acts 1:8).

Ministering to the Sick

One time I arrived in Cochin, South India one day earlier than the scheduled date. I booked into a hotel, and looking around I discovered a hospital across the street. I had a prompting of the Holy Spirit to visit the hospital and pray for the sick.

> "They went forth and preached everywhere, the Lord . . . confirming the Word with signs following"
>
> Mark 16:20

The head administrator gave me permission to pray for the sick who were everywhere, in the hallways and wherever there was room. I will never forget the response. The place came alive with faith and the Spirit of God. The people reached out with such eagerness to receive a touch from God.

You see, we are His extended hands reaching out to others. It says of the disciples, **"They went forth and preached everywhere, the Lord working with them, and confirming the Word with signs following" (Mark 16:20).** I thank God for the mix-up with the itinerary. God can break into my itinerary any time He needs to! Bless God, our times are in His hands.

It was a memorable moment in time that goes down in Heaven's records. Many were ministered to as we spoke the powerful Name of Jesus. There is no greater name in Heaven, on earth, or under the earth. There is power and authority in that Name. I was so happy leaving the hospital that day. I knew we had touched God and we were able to leave a blessing behind us. What a joy it is to be able to proclaim the mighty Name of Jesus to a perishing world. You don't have to be a great preacher to heal the sick; just have faith in a great God. What a thrill it is to deliver the healing power to the masses.

One time I was ministering to a large crowd and I felt a breeze of the Holy Spirit sweep over the people. They noticed it too as there was a response in the people. I knew it was a visitation of His presence. Scores of people that night testified to the healing power of God. It was amazing to see thousands crying out to Jesus to save them.

GODLY PARENTS

I thank God for my parents who obeyed God to be filled with the Holy Ghost. My family was asked to leave the Baptist Church we were attending. The pastor didn't know they were doing the will of God. Not long afterward, the whole family was all baptized in the Holy Ghost. I come from a wonderful family of six children. There was a price to pay but nothing in comparison to the blessing we came into. Getting filled with the Holy Ghost will transform your life and prepare you for a vibrant ministry.

I thank God for folk who will step out of the boat for more of Jesus. Jesus said, **"Ye shall receive power after that the Holy Ghost is come upon you" (Acts 1:8).** To deny the infilling of the Holy Ghost is to deny His power. He is the impetus we need, He is the strength we need, the anointing and the power. It will change you from the nominal to the phenomenal, from the ordinary to the extraordinary, from the natural to the supernatural, and from a spectator to a participator.

Chapter Nine

BEYOND FORGIVENESS

I remember a man of God saying that God does not just forgive us and put us on the road to eternity; He gives us a million dollars for the journey. He is a God of **"good measure, and pressed down, and shaken together, and running over" (Luke 6:38).** God is extravagant when it comes to His grace and mercy. David saw God as a God of plenty! He said things like:

"He hath dealt bountifully with me" (Ps. 13:6)
"My cup runneth over" (Ps. 23:5)
"(He is) plenteous in mercy" (Ps. 86:5)
"(He) daily loadeth us with benefits" (Ps. 68:19)

Let us take the account of the Good Samaritan. While on the dusty Jericho Road, he saw a poor man half dead, robbed, stripped, wounded, and bleeding. The Samaritan stopped and compassionately bound up his wounds and poured in oil and wine. He set him on his own beast and took him to the inn. The next day, he paid the innkeeper for the room, then said, **"Whatsoever thou spendest more, when I come again, I will repay thee" (Luke 10:30-35).** It proves that God's love goes the distance and then some! God spares no expense. He lavishes upon us with extravagance.

Each one of us was like the wounded man on the Jericho Road until Jesus found us and lovingly took care of us. He took us unto Himself and He poured in the oil and wine. You will notice that the Good Samaritan went the extra mile. He not only paid the bill but also told the innkeeper that should there be any more expense, he would take care of that too.

HIS PARDONING GRACE

Paul enlarges on the "riches of His grace" and on the "glory of His grace." He said that God has abounded toward us **(Phil. 1:6-8)!** When it says **"He hath <u>abounded</u> toward us" (Eph. 1:6-8)**, it means EXCEEDINGLY ABUNDANT. Peter asked the Master, **"How often shall my brother sin against me, and I forgive him? Till seven times?"** Jesus said unto him, **"I say not unto you until seven times, but seventy times seven!" (Mt. 18:21-23).**

God is not asking Peter to do anything that God doesn't do. The believer abides under the shadow of His forgiveness every minute of every day. His pardoning grace is abounding toward us and <u>covering us continually</u>. Child of God, He has nothing on you; He does not keep records as some might believe. The blood of Jesus Christ efficaciously cleanses us from all sin. The blood that flowed from Calvary cries out "FORGIVEN" on your behalf. It speaks on your behalf. God's forgiveness on behalf of His saints is around the clock! God said, **"When I see the blood, I will pass over you" (Ex. 12:13).**

> **"Of His fullness have all we received, and grace for grace"**
>
> **John 1:16**

This does not give us free rein to frustrate God's grace, but who desires to do that? God's grace is the believer's confidence that without it he could not walk in peace. Being under the blood fills the heart with the peace of the Holy Spirit.

Paul said, **"Grace be to you, and peace from God our Father" (Eph. 1:2).** Grace and peace just go together; they walk hand in hand. Those who do not enjoy the peace of God in their lives do not fully understand the wonderful work of God's amazing grace.

Since God's grace has placed you **"in Christ, (you are) a new creature" (2 Cor. 5:17)** – that is who you are! **"(He) is made unto us wisdom, and righteousness, and sanctification, and redemption" (1 Cor. 1:30).** Grace presents us to the Father washed in the blood of the Lamb. Grace presents us to God in the robe of righteousness. Grace presents us to God a redeemed, blood-bought child of God. God gave us His righteousness. It may take all the faith you have to believe it, yet it is true!

When we believe who God says we are, it will alter our whole perspective on life. You might say, "How can it be?" Paul said God did it **"according to His good pleasure" (Eph. 1:9).** It is true, we cannot say we deserve such kindness but that is why we sing

"Amazing Grace, how sweet the sound
That saved a wretch like me
I once was lost but now I'm found
Was blind, but now I see."

John the Beloved Disciple said, ". . . **we beheld His glory, the glory as of the only begotten of the Father, full of grace and truth . . . of His fullness have all we received, and grace for grace" (John 1:14-16).** Think about that for a moment. God doesn't just have grace, but He is FULL of grace and truth. The meaning of the word "full" is "covered over" or "complete."

HIS BOUNTIFUL GOODNESS

I was flying with a missionary friend from Texas in his Mooney airplane when he asked me what I thought of the verse that says we received GRACE FOR GRACE. I likened it to a McDonald's Big Mac -- like stack upon stack of the good stuff! We have all heard of those piled high hamburgers! Well, as crude as the illustration was, he began to laugh and rejoice. Child of God, God has blessed us with GRACE UPON

GRACE. **"And of His fullness have all we received"** **(John 1:16).** Isn't that wonderful?

My friend, sit back and enjoy the journey. Rejoice in the finished work of the cross on your behalf. Many endure it instead of enjoying it. God wants us to enjoy Him and praise Him for His bountiful goodness toward us.

An ocean liner took its passengers to a beautiful tropical island. It took several days of travel. When they arrived at their destination, a man noticed that his friend had been missing most of the journey. "Oh," his friend said, "I just stayed in my cabin, and when it came meal time, I just ate the cheese and crackers I brought with me." His friend pointed out to him that the ticket he had purchased entitled him to full dining rights and the rights to every deck and luxury the ship afforded.

Many folk are like this man, confined to their cabin, eating their cheese and crackers when God has a place set for them on the upper deck. They are content with crumbs while filet mignon is being served. The Bible tells us, **"The blessing of the Lord, it maketh rich, and He addeth no sorrow with it" (Prov. 10:22).**

ALL WE NEED IS JESUS

Child of God, your Heavenly Father wants you to so enjoy Him, to bask in the sunshine and warmth of His love. It is His will that we <u>GROW</u> in His grace (favour). You are <u>COMPLETE</u> in Christ; He has made you <u>WHOLE</u>! You are a <u>NEW</u> <u>CREATION</u>, adopted into the family of God.

His abundant grace has you covered from head to toe. Religions of today have themselves covered with earthly garb; mankind seeks to cover themselves as Adam and Eve did in the Garden, but their covering is inadequate and insufficient to save and mask their nakedness. Material robes and garments are man's way of being religious and endeavoring to display his spirituality when all of the time, God looks on the HEART and NOT THE OUTWARD APPEARANCE.

There is nothing we can do to earn God's acceptance. Jesus is our covering, our sanctification, our righteousness, our salvation, our security. We don't need any add-ons or extensions – only Jesus! Paul said, **"A Jew (is one who) is one INWARDLY" (Rom. 2:29). "For with the HEART man BELIEVETH unto righteousness" (Rom. 10:10).** It is what we have in our hearts – the faith, the trust, and reliance on Him that separates us unto God. Jesus did everything possible to make us whole and to bring us to a place of completeness. There's simply nothing left to do but lift up holy hands and praise Him.

GRAFTED IN

Can you see it? "Jesus is made unto us . . ." Every believer is a partaker (partner) of His DIVINE NATURE; we have been grafted into the vine. His fullness is flowing into you. The life of His Spirit is coursing through your veins. There is a transfusion going on; His life and nature are being divinely imparted into your spirit. Through the "New Birth" we are divinely connected to the heavenly calling, we are JOINED unto the Lord. Isn't that wonderful?

Chapter Ten

YOU SHALL RECEIVE POWER

When I was just a lad, a man of God visited our small church in the town of Booker Bay, just north of Sydney. After he preached, he invited every person who desired to be filled with the Holy Spirit to join him in the back room of the church. Many folks responded including me. After he prayed, the Holy Spirit, as in Bible days, fell on us and we were saturated in the Holy Spirit's blessing. We began worshipping and praising the Lord in other tongues as they did on the Day of Pentecost **(Acts 2:1-4).**

> **"Ye shall receive power, after that the Holy Ghost is come upon you; and ye shall be witnesses unto me both in Jerusalem, and in all Judaea, and in Samaria, and unto the uttermost part of the earth"**
>
> **Acts 1:8**

I can never forget the impact this experience had on my young life. I lost all track of time and realized that it was dark when we came out of the room. I had been literally flooded with the presence of God, and I knew that I had touched Him.

For countless weeks the cloud of His presence was over my life. It was like Jesus got a hold of my life and He wouldn't let me go. The reality of His love burst in upon my soul. Jesus said, **"Out of your belly (innermost being) shall flow rivers of living water" (John 7:38).** I knew the power of God had invaded my life as it promised in Scripture. **"And it shall come to pass in** the last days, saith God, I will pour out my Spirit upon all flesh" (Acts 2:17, quoted from Joel 2:28).

Looking back, I can see God's hand on my life, preparing me for the work and ministry He called me to. For Jesus said, **"Ye shall receive power, after that the Holy Ghost is come upon you; and ye shall be witnesses unto me both in Jerusalem, and in all Judaea, and in Samaria, and unto the uttermost part of the earth" (Acts 1:8).**

FOR EVERYONE

The Word of God makes it so clear that the promise of this gift is for all of God's children. **"The promise is unto you, and to your children, and to all that are afar off, even as many as the Lord our God shall call" (Acts 2:39).** Yes, this phenomenon is for everyone: every believer, every child of God, male or female, boy or girl. God is no respecter of persons; what He has done for others, He will surely do for you.

After a five-day open-air crusade in south India, we conducted a believers' meeting for the new converts. We witnessed many of these precious people being filled with the Holy Spirit. God poured out His Spirit upon them, filling them with the fire of God. The people we lead to Christ must not be denied this blessed infilling of the Holy Ghost, for Jesus said, **"You shall receive power after that the Holy Ghost is come upon you" (Acts 1:8).** We must send them off into the world with **power** for the journey, and strength for their way.

Dynamite

The baptism of the Holy Spirit was given that the believer might have **power** for service. He said that we would be His witnesses. The word "power" comes from the Greek word "*dunamis*" from which we derive the word "dynamite," meaning "miraculous power," "ability," "strength," "abundance," and "wonderful work." This wonderful experience is for those who are dry and thirsty; those who possess a longing for more of God's fullness and a rich anointing of His power and strength. Jesus said, **"If any man thirst, let him come unto Me and drink" (John 7:37).**

God's Word refers to us as vessels which denotes that we are to be filled. It says of the apostle Stephen that he was **"a man full of faith and of the Holy Ghost . . . (and) did mighty wonders and miracles among the people" (Acts 6:5-6).**

Heavenly Experience

The baptism of the Holy Spirit is a supernatural experience from Heaven. It was Heaven-sent **(Acts 2:2).** We give the Holy Spirit the right to speak through us. The Word tells us, **"They were all filled with the Holy Ghost, and began to speak with other tongues as the Spirit gave them utterance" (Acts 2:4).** They were speaking the wonderful works of God **(vs. 11).** Oh, how we need the Holy Spirit to take control of our tongues! The Holy Spirit is the only One Who can tame our tongues and bring them into submission to the will of God. We must yield to the Spirit of God **"for we know not what we should pray for as we ought, but the Spirit (Himself) makes intercession for us" (Rom. 8:26).** Speaking the language of the Spirit of God is the most wonderful asset the believer can posess. What a blessing, what a foretaste of glory divine! **"For he that speaketh in an unknown tongue speaketh not unto men, but unto God . . . howbeit in the Spirit, he speaketh mysteries" (1 Cor. 14:2).**

References to the Holy Spirit's outpouring are evidenced throughout the ministry of the early apostles. It seems that everywhere they went, the gift of the Holy Spirit was poured out on the people. Here are some references: **Acts 10:44-46; Acts 11:15-17; Acts 19:1-6.**

THE RIVER OF GOD

We can serve God in our own way standing on the bank of the river. We can even step into God's river and still serve Him. But there is a river out there that cannot be crossed, with waters to swim in **(Ezek. 47:5)** out there where deep channels of His abundant blessings are supernaturally flowing. The Holy Spirit beckons us to a deeper walk in the Spirit, an experience that surpasses the normal and ordinary, into the realm of His miracle power and His anointing.

> **"We have this treasure in earthen vessels, that the excellency of the power may be of God, and not of us"**
>
> **2 Cor. 4:7**

The baptism of the Holy Spirit is a gift from God. Therefore it must be good! Millions around the world have received the gift with the evidence of speaking with other tongues. It is a divine encounter with the presence and glory of our Heavenly Father.

Are you ready, child of God? Are you ready to be empowered, clothed upon with **power from on high?** Bring your empty vessel to Him and allow Him to saturate your life with the fullness of His blessing.

THE FIRE OF GOD

In Old Testament times, they brought a sacrifice unto God. A lamb was placed on the altar and it became a burnt offering, consumed with fire **(Lev. 1:7-13).** Oh, how we need to be consumed with the Holy Spirit of God. It is not enough to be saved and on our way to Heaven. It is imperative that we be baptized with the Holy Ghost and with fire. A fire experience is what every believer needs. John the Baptist said, **"He**

(Jesus) shall baptize you with the Holy Ghost, and
with fire" (Mt. 3:11; Acts 2:3).

God touched the lips of the prophet Isaiah with a live coal
from off His altar (Is. 6:5-7). Nothing can take the place of
the precious anointing of the Holy Spirit. Jesus said, "You
shall receive power after that the Holy Ghost is
come upon you" (Acts 1:8).

Are You Thirsty?

Friend, are you hungry? Are you thirsty for His fullness?
Jesus declared, "Blessed are they which do hunger and
thirst after righteousness, for they shall be filled"
(Mt. 5:6). Are you ready to step into the river of His
fullness? Are you ready to have a richer and fuller prayer
life? Do you desire to be a bolder witness for the Lord? Do
you want the power of God in your ministry? Then this
outpouring is what you need.

"I will pour
water upon him
that is thirsty,
and floods upon
the dry ground"

(Is. 44:3).

The Holy Spirit is given to the
believer for his own edification and
for his effectiveness for the
Kingdom of God. The baptism of
the Holy Spirit is an immersion into
the fullness of God's anointing.

If you are on the path of "more of
God", it will lead you to the river of
God. It is there that you will be
immersed in the refreshing, living
water of His Spirit. God said, "I will pour water upon
him that is thirsty, and floods upon the dry ground"
(Is. 44:3).

Clean Before the Lord

God has been pouring out His Holy Spirit ever since the Day of Pentecost; that miraculous stream is still flowing today. It is still making people whole and filling them with the power of God. It is still clothing them with power from on high and bringing them into the supernatural ability of God.

To be filled with His heavenly endowment of power, you don't have to be perfect, just clean before Him. Jesus is the baptizer in the Holy Spirit. It is so simple; just ask Him to wash you from all of your sin. This prepares you to be filled with the new wine of the Spirit.

HELPFUL INSTRUCTIONS

- While in His presence, yield yourself to Jesus.

- Release your faith and ask Him to fill you with His Holy Spirit.

- Relax, and begin worshipping Him out of your heart of love.

- Praise Him with your lips.

- Center your attention on Jesus alone! You will sense His Spirit flowing through you.

- At that time, the Holy Spirit will cause you to speak in your new heavenly language.

- When you do, don't stop.

- Allow the river to flow through you.

Photos

The Idaho Falls Christian Center began with the ministry of Cliff and Helen Beard, and then was pastored for ten years by Tim and Carole-Anne Marsh. The church witnessed a wonderful move of God's Holy Spirit throughout the Snake River Valley.

Family picture taken in Swan Valley, Idaho: Carole-Anne, Tim, Julie-Anne, Rebecca, David, and Jonathan.

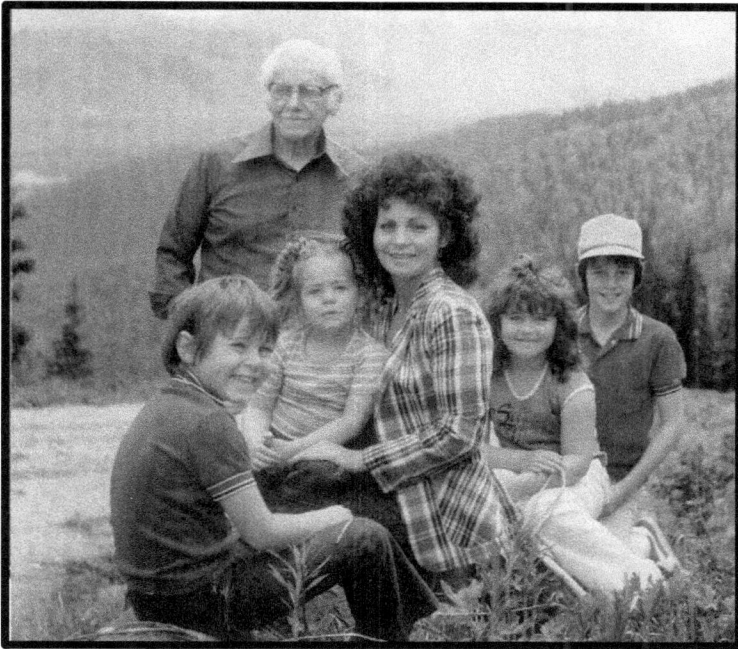

Family picture in Jackson, Wyoming, including Grandpa Marsh.

My wife, Carole-Anne and
our grandchildren.

Our two grandchildren, Isaiah and
Caleb.

Thousands of people gather nightly in S. India to hear the preaching of God's Word and to receive the miracle touch of His power.

The Holy Spirit is moving upon these people as they receive Christ into their lives . . . you can see it on their faces.

With hands lifted, we teach the people to reach out and receive from God.

Hungry hearts are gathering on a street in S. India as we share Jesus with them.

The city of Punnapra, S. India: thousands came to receive a miracle from God. There is wonder working power in the cross of Calvary.

Rev. V. A. Thampy, President of The New India Church of God, has been remarkably used of God for forty years. It has been a joy to work with his foundation throughout the years.

This boat was a gift to the work and ministry of V. A. Thampy by the Idaho Falls Christian Center. The boat was a powerful tool for reaching the unreached throughout the backwaters of S. India.

Tim Marsh and David Gourley of Missouri team up for revival meetings throughout India and Sri Lanka.

If this book has blessed you, please let us know.
It would make a great gift for a friend.

Tim Marsh Ministries
P. O. Box 1351, Torrance, CA 90505
timmarshusa@gmail.com

Printed in the USA

www.ingramcontent.com/pod-product-compliance
Lightning Source LLC
LaVergne TN
LVHW021522080426
835509LV00018B/2618